WOMEN, FOOD, AND DESIRE

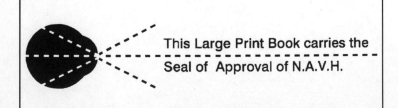

This Large Print Book carries the
Seal of Approval of N.A.V.H.

WOMEN, FOOD, AND DESIRE

EMBRACE YOUR CRAVINGS, MAKE PEACE WITH FOOD, RECLAIM YOUR BODY

ALEXANDRA JAMIESON

THORNDIKE PRESS
A part of Gale, Cengage Learning

GALE
CENGAGE Learning

Farmington Hills, Mich • San Francisco • New York • Waterville, Maine
Meriden, Conn • Mason, Ohio • Chicago

GALE
CENGAGE Learning®

Thorndike Press® Large Print Health, Home & Learning.
The text of this Large Print edition is unabridged.
Other aspects of the book may vary from the original edition.
Set in 16 pt. Plantin.

LIBRARY OF CONGRESS CATALOGING-IN-PUBLICATION DATA

Jamieson, Alexandra, 1975–
    Women, food, and desire : embrace your cravings, make peace with food, reclaim your body / by Alexandra Jamieson. — Large print edition.
    pages cm. — (Thorndike press large print health, home & learning)
    ISBN 978-1-4104-7787-3 (hardcover) — ISBN 1-4104-7787-8 (hardcover)
    1. Women—Psychology. 2. Self-actualization (Psychology) 3. Women—Nutrition. 4. Body image. I. Title.
    HQ1206.J365 2015
    155.3'33—dc23   2014047737

Published in 2015 by arrangement with Gallery Books, a division of Simon & Schuster, Inc.

Printed in Mexico
1 2 3 4 5 6 7 19 18 17 16 15

To my friends and family,
who have always supported
my evolving search for my truth.

To every client and reader who has
heard the cravings of their soul for
health and happiness, and
invited me into their journey.
Let's shamelessly declare
our desires together.

For my mother,
Annabeth Eve Parker Jamieson

For Annie Fox, friend and mentor

Your body is precious. It is our vehicle for awakening. Treat it with care.

— Buddha

The old are kind. The young are hot. Love may be blind. Desire is not.

— Leonard Cohen

CONTENTS

INTRODUCTION:
TAPPING INTO DESIRE

Fear is a natural reaction to moving
closer to the truth.
— Pema Chödrön

What do you want?

This may seem like a simple, even child-ish question, but I believe it's the essential question of every woman's life. And yet, sadly, it's one we infrequently ask each other, and even more rarely, ourselves. It's a dangerous question for many of us, because it's asking us to get really honest with who we are and to be willing to share that truth with others. I know from my own experience that getting to those huge, life-defining points in my life where I had no option but to ask myself this question — and be willing to accept the answer — were huge turning points for me. When I finally built up the courage to address this issue with brutal honesty, I found myself moving from doubt

11

to deepening self-trust. I was accepting my own true power as a woman, and each time I did this, my life immediately became more vibrant, more potent, more passionate.

As I mature, I'm less frightened when this question arises, because I've finally had enough experience to know that when I'm pressed to be honest this way, good things are coming. And because I want other women to experience the breakthroughs that can only come with tapping into their desires, I've made it my life's work to look deeply into the eyes of others and ask: What is it that your heart most desires? The answers run the gamut from, "I want to lose twenty-five pounds" to "I want to meet my life partner," or "I want to break my addiction to sugar" to "I want to regain my power and ability to make a positive impact on the world." This is the beauty of my work as a functional nutrition coach. My role is to be a reliable, knowledgeable, and trustworthy support to each woman as she finds her way back into her heart and body so she can feel alive and whole again.

When I first pose this question to a new client, it's not uncommon for her to cry, even if we're meeting for the first time. That's because this question is bursting with such deep meaning that it often bypasses the head and goes right to the heart. Plus, it's a bit of a shock when someone else asks this question with no agenda other than genuine interest. When someone wants to know what our most secret wishes for ourselves are, we immediately become exquisitely vulnerable. We immediately become seen. And if we truthfully answer the question, then — and most terrifying of all — we become known.

Being seen and truly known can scare us enough to cause us to avoid desire. It's easier, or so it seems, to be good, compliant, pleasing to others. But living this way doesn't satisfy us. Many of us spend too much time trying to be something we're not or what someone else wants us to be, so this question just gets swept under the rug of a busy life. Yet every one of us — regardless of our age, our weight, our relationship status, or how much money we have in the bank — deserves to ask ourselves this question and then answer it with action. Because if we don't ask and answer this question, then what exactly are we doing here?

Feeling good is the primary intention.
— Danielle LaPorte

The next question we need to ask ourselves is: How do I want to feel? Women come to me because they don't feel good. They feel uncomfortable in their own bodies for a vast array of reasons, but most of those reasons boil down to having lost the ability to trust oneself.

Many women can only identify this lack of self-trust as it relates to how they look or how they feel. When someone is feeling heavy enough or tired enough or deprived of touch or sex or laughter or sunlight, that's when the instinct for self-preservation usually kicks in and a step is taken to get better. This is when the questions can be asked — and answered. And the first question I usually hear is, "How can I become more comfortable around food?"

THE OTHER F-WORD

I'm a big believer that aside from providing us with the nutritional fuel we need to function at our best, food should make us happy. That's right: food should delight us, ignite us, and make us feel good. Really, really good.

But for most of us, the way we approach food does just the opposite. It makes us feel fat. It makes us feel ashamed. It makes us feel ugly and undesirable. It makes us feel wrong and unwelcome in our own bodies.

And when we lose our knowledge that we have power over our relationship to it, it allows us to hide out from life.

Food, in our current culture, has become the other F-word; most of our interactions with it fill us with shame, guilt, and discomfort. When we eat, and especially when we overeat or eat things we know are bad for us, we tend to gobble our food as though it's some kind of necessary evil that needs to be gotten through as swiftly as possible. Eating fast is the most culturally acceptable way to do it (why else do they call it "fast food"?).

But our relationship with food isn't meant to be so "fast" and furtive. What if we were to let ourselves slow down? What if we really aimed to have a relationship with food that honored how complex and ever-changing our needs and our lives are? What if we decided that we would approach our relationship to food from a place of honor and awareness rather than one of shame and guilt? What if we committed to a practice of eating mindfully and actually tasting — and experiencing — each bite of food we take? What if we cared enough about our bodies to want to be really present whenever we fed them?

These are the questions we need to ask

ourselves about our relationship to food if we're ever going to make radical adjustments to the way we eat. We need to shine our awareness on how our bodies feel around and with food and how we'd like them to feel. When we do this, we realize we are not powerless over food, and then we can begin to look at our eating habits with curiosity. Only then can we change our relationship with food.

But there's more. This isn't the only relationship crying out for attention. There are other cravings we need to meet, too. What about our desires for meaningful work, liberating play, satisfying sex, companionship, intellectual stimulation, rest? All of these yearnings, just like those for food, should be met with deep, abiding self-respect and playful curiosity. Otherwise, we'll stay trapped by our cravings, which keep us too distracted to take notice of our deepest, most truthful desires.

We lose a fragile quality of spirit when we overeat, undersleep, don't play enough, don't have enough sex or intimate physical contact, or spend our days doing unfulfilling work. We resign ourselves to "not having" and "not deserving," and lose our connection to our deepest self. When we're no longer attuned to ourselves, then we tend to over- or underrespond — especially with food — and this just keeps us off-balance and unwell. When we aren't attentive to how we're feeling, our reactions tend to be extreme. This is when we let our cravings control us. And when we blindly follow our cravings, without asking what they mean, it's like applying a blunt hammer when what's required is a feather's touch. When we don't listen to the message behind our cravings, we lose all sense of nuance and measure — all of the qualities that are at the heart of female desire. When we're at a craving's mercy, it's impossible to really listen to ourselves, to hear what we really need.

WHY WE HIDE BEHIND OUR CRAVINGS

From craving is born grief, from craving is born fear. For one freed from craving there is no grief — so how fear?
— Buddha

Chocoholics will describe a favorite cake in rapturous detail. Cheese lovers moan in ecstasy when recalling warm Brie. Our favorite food cravings can put us in an incredibly heightened state of pleasure because they have the power to activate our senses in a way that is tough to match. When we indulge in what we love best, we can experience full mind-body rapture. But there can be too much of a good thing, as all of us who've felt crippled by our cravings know.

Without really knowing that we're even doing it, many of us tend to disappear into our cravings. When we're battling the pull of the artisanal ice cream or the luscious designer coffee drink, we relinquish our attention to how we are actually feeling. Cravings are so easy to hide out in because they distance us from our ability to see beyond the immediate hit of satisfaction, and they set us up to engage in habits that keep us down and out of touch with ourselves. Then the cycle of craving takes over.

If we're busily distracted, riding the carnival ride of cravings, we don't have to do the work of looking after ourselves. That's the unspoken benefit of hiding out in the craving cave: it keeps us from having to engage in active, meaningful self-care.

But there are ways to break this cycle, to get out from under the spell of cravings. And in this book, we'll explore many ways of finding the courage to pause, stand free and clear, and think differently about what will bring you lasting pleasure. You will discover the ability to live happily in your body, just as it is right now. It's time to find out what you really want, what you truly desire.

HOW OUR CRAVINGS CAN SAVE US

We eat the way we eat because we are afraid to feel what we feel.
— Geneen Roth

Ah, the siren song of forbidden foods. We all know it. We're feeling out of sorts and so we turn to food for solace. We eat, and while we're eating, we're distracted from what we're feeling, so we experience a moment of relief. But when we've demolished the cookies and thrown away the bag, what are we left with? We're left with our unmet needs and a sugar high that will quickly turn into a sugar hangover. So the craving rises again, calling out to us "Feed me!" and again we take the easy route and stuff it back down with food. We try desperately to drown our feelings by eating instead of listening. This habit — and it is a habit — of caving into our cravings before we've examined them has left us all feeling heavy, tired, lonely, and stuck at some time or another in our lives.

But what if we learned to listen to our cravings? What if we learned to ask ourselves this question before we just gave in: What do I really want? What if we could just sit in our discomfort while the answer came to us? Then we might find that what we think we crave and what we really want are two very different things.

When we can honestly listen to the wisdom of our cravings, magical, life-altering things can happen. When we respect our cravings for what they are — deep messages from our soul — real transformation is possible. And when we're no longer slaves to our cravings, then our truest and deepest desires can float up from our hearts. Then — if we are willing to be vulnerable, shaky, scared, open, and brave — we can fulfill them.

WHY WE HAVE TO FAIL TO SUCCEED
My life has been a series of what I call "successful failures." Until my midtwenties, I changed career paths three or four times, looking for the one I thought would make me feel the most passionate and engaged. Each time, I threw myself wholeheartedly into the work, and I gave each job at least one full year, thinking that I needed this

much time to become properly trained and to find out if the work was right for me.

After working for a year as an assistant media planner for one of the biggest advertising agencies in the world, I realized I didn't care about Clorox; I didn't even use bleach, so why would I want to spend my time selling it to other people? I started talking to my friends about their plans and jobs, and I ran into a college buddy who was moving to Lake Tahoe to work at a ski resort. After a weekend visit and checking out the resort's job listings, I knew I wanted to leave the city and head for the mountains, where I could spend most of my time outdoors. My heart was saying that I wanted to be a ski bum, not a corporate drone. I was scared to death to tell my parents that I was quitting the great job I'd worked so hard to get. My dad had even helped me pay for my move to San Francisco, buying me the plane ticket for the interview that got me the job. Would he see me as a quitter? A failure? I thought about this, but realized that my dad would likely support my move, because even though I was giving up the trappings of success (the requisite work clothes, the daily commute), I would be making virtually the same money working at the ski resort.

I had to live with that fear until I made a decision. I spent a lot of time doubting myself and beating myself up, but once I gave notice and began the work of redefining my life, I found myself feeling much more energized and excited about the future. I was surprised that I also felt much more confident. I was beginning to learn that by checking things off my list of possibilities and trying new things, I was moving closer to being my true self. Saying no to the things that don't feel right is as important as saying yes to the ones that do.

Since then, every time I've left a job, a city, or even a partner, when I step into that vast unknown, wide-open space, I can count on something magical happening.

This is the space of possibility that exists for all of us. But we can only get there when we resist the cravings that keep us stuck in the habits of thought and action that are no longer working for us.

For me, this "in-between space" was, and still is, a place of deep physical knowing. Once I make the decision to change, my body responds with cues that say "Yes, good! Do that!" Every time I take one step in the next right direction, no matter how small that step may be, I leave staying stuck in a funk behind. I step out of habit and into possibility.

So I moved up to Lake Tahoe and got a job in a beautiful Sierra resort in the conference-planning department. I had always loved party planning, and the entry-level position took advantage of these skills, plus, the job provided me with full benefits and a ski pass. I was also surrounded by handsome, twenty-something ski bums who, while in the best physical shape of their lives, spent most of their free time smoking pot and snowboarding. Hanging out with them was fun for a few months, but "the life," as they called it, got old for me pretty quickly.

But I put in my time and after a year of lugging boxes full of binders for retreat meetings, dating "snow dudes," and dealing with stressed-out conference coordinators, I realized event planning wasn't my life's calling, so I moved to New York City, where my brother lived. I stayed in a spare room in his office in the East Village for a few months while I worked as the day bartender at a famous Irish pub on St. Mark's Place. This was an incredibly trendy spot, and I spent my days pulling pints for famous writers and actors. But before long, my body was getting that itchy feeling, that impulse to quite literally get out. Tending bar in the dark while the sun was shining began to turn my brain to mush, so I applied for a position as a legal assistant at an entertainment law firm.

You've heard sitting is the new smoking, right? Well, in my case, working at a corporate desk job turned out to be downright deadly. At the law firm where I worked, I sat in artificial lighting at a desk with a chair that gave me terrible backaches. I was not allowed Internet access because as an assistant, I might "abuse" the privilege. (I guess this rule didn't apply to the partner I caught watching porn on his computer.) Ten-hour workdays were the norm, not the exception. I had toyed with the idea of applying to law school, but after a few months of long days and passionless work, I started to feel so physically awful that all I could think about was what I needed to do to get better. I was suffering from migraine headaches, almost daily, and I was going through handfuls of Advil in a failed attempt to dull the pain. I was depressed and exhausted, even after sleeping ten to twelve hours a night on weekends. My back was a wreck and I was eating candy bars and pastries and drinking caffeine all day in an attempt to manage all of this discomfort.

I finally went to a doctor because the

headaches were getting out of hand. My mother's stories of her sister's and father's suicides by overdose and their abuse of painkillers haunted me every time I took another two or three Advil, and I knew that having so many headaches meant that something was really wrong. Within minutes of sitting in the doctor's examination room, after I briefly explained my symptoms, the doctor handed me two pieces of paper: one was a prescription for painkillers and the other one was for Prozac. I froze. Everything in my body said, "I don't want prescriptions to mask the pain. I need to heal!"

I left the doctor's office with the prescriptions in my purse, but with no intention of filling them. Instead, I asked around and got a recommendation for a more holistic doctor, who agreed to see me the next day. Sitting in the waiting room at his office, I looked around at the Buddha statue, a tinkling waterfall, and live ferns that were growing beside a display of nutritional supplements. This didn't feel like any doctor's office I'd ever visited before, but there were diplomas on the walls, too, so I felt at least a little reassured. A nurse showed me to the exam room, and I sat on the examination table and waited.

The doctor came in and sat across from

me. He introduced himself and asked me to describe my concerns. After a few minutes, he asked me what I was eating. I was a bit shocked. No doctor had ever asked me that question before. I described my diet: croissant and a skinny vanilla latte in the morning, fast food from Subway or McDonald's with a soda for lunch (the two-cheeseburger meal was my favorite), and Chinese takeout or pasta for dinner.

"No wonder you're sick. Your diet is totally refined and that's what is causing your headaches." He explained how the sugar and all the additives in refined foods were causing an overgrowth of candida, a yeast, in my body and thereby causing the headaches. Before I left, he handed me a list of foods I ought to eat (fresh, plant-based foods) and those I ought to avoid (dairy, coffee, sugar, wheat, corn, meat), and he suggested some vitamins I might take to help replace the nutrients my diet had been lacking.

No sugar? No caffeine? No McDonald's? This doctor was suggesting that I needed to eliminate about 75 percent of what I was currently eating in order to feel better. To say that these recommendations scared me is an understatement: I felt completely overwhelmed. But I felt so awful I was willing to try anything, so I left his office and went to the library to get some books on the subject. I found cookbooks that focused on this new, "clean" style of eating and also several books on nutrition for health. As I dug around, I began to realize that there were whole sections of the library devoted to healthy eating.

I started by stripping out the easy things, like pastries and fast food and deluxe designer coffees. But soon I went beyond the doctor's recommendation and started eating a 100 percent plant-based diet. Within a week or two, my entire body began to change. The headaches stopped. My depression and exhaustion disappeared. I started to feel focused, light, and strong again. And the twenty-five extra pounds I had put on since I left my ski resort job melted off over the course of a few months, without my even noticing. Then, I woke up one day and I realized I felt *amazing*!

I knew if I was going to make this miracle diet stick, I'd have to learn how to do more than toss a salad with tofu. I found the Natural Gourmet Institute, a culinary school in Manhattan that offered evening and weekend classes using mostly plant-based ingredients. I signed up and took a basic cooking class over a weekend. By the end of the class, I was hooked. The idea that maybe I could create this kind of food for a living bubbled up inside me and I asked for information on the professional training program that the school offered.

With help from my father and stepmom, I took out another student loan, quit my legal job, and started culinary school. Over the next thirteen years, I helped conceive and make the Oscar-nominated documentary *Super Size Me,* earned a certification from the Institute for Integrative Nutrition, and published three nutrition books. I appeared in countless magazines, on news programs, and in documentaries sharing my story and my newfound perspective on food. I hung out with the "big vegans" in New York City, and spoke on stages about vegan parenting. I was married to a famous filmmaker, traveled the world, and walked the red carpet by his side.

And then it all came tumbling down. Soon after our son was born, I discovered that I couldn't trust my husband, so we began counseling. The therapist made little headway in helping us heal our broken bond, and we began a long and slow divorce process. I felt like a complete failure. My career was floundering, my marriage was over, and I was now a single mom. Something in my body began to shift, and my menstrual cycle started cycling faster; I started getting my period every fourteen to sixteen days. I was crampy, depleted, and exhausted, and I was miserable.

And I started to crave meat. And sex. I hadn't had either in so long that the feelings of discomfort that these cravings triggered in me were impossible to identify for many months. I would find myself wandering the aisles of the grocery store looking for something to satisfy this deep wanting, but I couldn't figure out what it was.

One day I walked into my super-hippie grocery co-op in Brooklyn and wandered around for ten minutes with an empty basket. I must have looked like a crazy homeless lady, because I'd just dropped off my son at preschool and hadn't showered in days. Wearing stretched-out yoga pants, shuffling and mumbling as I looked for something, *anything,* to satisfy me, I left without buying a thing. I had picked up chocolate, ice cream, chips, and even kale, but nothing *felt* like what I wanted.

I wanted — I needed — something, but I just couldn't put my finger on what that something was.

Around this time, I was out to dinner with a couple of friends in Manhattan and they ordered steak and fish. I got the vegan pasta dish, with tofu and greens, a glass of wine, and a nice gazpacho. As our main courses arrived, my eyes rested on the meats placed before my friends. My torso and forehead became hot and yearning. My mouth started to water. I wanted to eat their meat.

This was bad.

I wasn't supposed to want meat! I was a vegan health counselor, for God's sake! I tried to ignore this "disgusting" feeling and focused on my pasta and drinking more wine. The talk turned to romance and my friends gently asked if I was ready to date. As I had been doing, I protested that it was too soon. This was the story I'd been telling myself for a while, and when my friends nodded in sympathetic understanding, I became annoyed. I was annoyed that they didn't try to talk me out of this idea, and annoyed that their food looked way better than mine.

I wanted meatballs. And I wanted a man.

One night around this time I was digging through my underwear drawer and rediscovered my vibrator. I hadn't used it in so long that at first I wasn't quite sure what it was doing there. I stood there, bewildered, until I felt a tingle of recognition that, while distant, was unmistakable. My body was telling me that it wanted to play, even though my brain didn't want to acknowledge this. Fortunately, I listened to my body instead of my brain. I found some fresh batteries, and I got busy.

All of these frustrations and "dead ends" were really opportunities for me to ask myself what I wanted. Career doesn't interest you? What do you want? Town too small? Where do you want to live? Relationship not stable or fulfilling? What kind of person do you want to be with? What is it that will feel good to you?

Are you willing to try again? And again, and again?

Yes. The answer has always been, will always be, *yes.*

Because every time I have tried something new, I learn something essential. Try a new man? I get to learn what your body likes and how to ask for what I want. Try a new diet? I discover what foods I am addicted or sensitive to and let them go. Try a new job? Learn a new job skill? I get to find new, more fulfilling work, a more supportive network, a more meaningful career.

And what if I "fail"? What if the boyfriend, the diet, or the job don't work out? Then I've still gained some invaluable information about what I need. I'm gathering the data I need to get closer to what I really want. The trick is to be ready to try again. Because every time I have taken the risk of finding out who I really am and what I really want, I've moved one step closer to being there.

This practice of saying yes to my yearnings, cravings, and desires has brought me full circle to a life and body I love. I listen to "her," my body. I ask her what she really needs. Every meal is an opportunity to have a conversation with myself about which foods will help me feel good — not just now, in this moment, but for the next few hours, the next few days, or in years to come. I don't engage in exercise as a way to burn off calories or punish myself for last night's dessert; now I take advantage of those times when I can move and stretch in ways that make me feel strong, relaxed, and sexy. How I spend my time, what I eat, what work I do, who I spend time with now matches up with how I want to feel. And how I want to feel is safe, sexy, and free, shamelessly. Join me.

CHAPTER ONE:
WHAT DO YOU CRAVE?

crav·ing
'krāvING/
noun
noun: craving; plural noun: cravings
1. a powerful desire for something

We all have cravings. Every single one of us human beings longs to connect with the people and things that will make us feel whole, alive, loved, and satisfied. I'd say, in fact, that this whole human experience of ours is essentially built on a bedrock of craving. It's human nature, after all, to yearn, to long, to want, to desire.

So I ask you, with genuine curiosity, genuine interest: What do you most crave?

I'm certain that it's not really that peanut butter cup you've got tucked away in the glove compartment of your car, or the triple venti latte with a shot of syrup that you rely on every afternoon to get you through another stressful day on the job.

I bet it's not that glass of wine you automatically reach for to help you relax at the end of a long, hard day. Nor is it the cookies, cakes, and other goodies you spend far too much time daydreaming about.

It's not the impulse to run away from your partner, or to yell at your kids, or to impetuously quit the job that is wrong for you — though we've all certainly had these moments, too.

What I want to know is what lies underneath all of these itchy, uncomfortable feelings? What incredibly important and vital needs of yours are going unmet, unacknowledged, unfed? What are you not getting from your food, your environment, your *life,* that makes you think you have no option but to overeat, overwork, act out, isolate, or overspend?

In other words, what do you most desire? What will make you feel most passionately alive? These are, I believe, the most important questions we can ask ourselves, and the answers are to be found in our cravings.

Whatever you need, it's rarely something that money can buy, but it is — and will continue to be — profoundly influenced by what you put into your mouth, what you do with your days, and what you either say or leave unsaid. If you've come to the point where what you're feeding yourself or telling yourself is filling, but not fulfilling, well, that means that the message buried beneath that craving just hasn't gotten through to you yet.

What most of my clients want is to feel radiantly alive and well. They want to wake up each day and step into their lives from a deeply authentic and honest place and know that the actions they take, the decisions they make, will truly reflect their most heartfelt values. They want to really believe, way down in their deepest soul, that they are valuable and worthwhile and that their choices matter. The key to achieving this profound level of comfort with the self is simple: learn to listen to your cravings. Listen to them, and learn to honor them. This is easy, but it is the hardest thing you will ever learn to do, because it takes putting yourself first in ways that are radically new, even frightening, for most of us. But it's time. It is time to stop mindlessly trying to get our cravings to stop bugging us. The irony here is that they will only loosen their grip on us when we commit to stop, listen, and learn from them. Only when you do this, when you learn to stop reacting and get quiet and really listen, will your cravings become what they truly are: your greatest guide.

In this book, I will teach you how to listen to your cravings. I will help you make peace with your body and your heart so you can truly, finally be at ease in the world. Because, in the end, that's what we women really crave: to belong, to be loved, to be well, especially within ourselves. We all want to know, really know, that we are perfect human beings, with no limitations on how we get to look, whom we get to love, what kind of contributions we'll decide to make in our lives. We've lost enough time battling our bodies, giving in to the societal pressure that says we have to look or be or eat "just so," and we've done this by hiding our truth from ourselves and everyone else around us. We've been cowering in shame long enough.

It's time. It's time for us all to lay down our weapons of self-destruction. It's time for us to become the exquisite caretakers of our own deepest desires.

In order to do this, we need to understand, respect, and embrace our cravings.

CRAVINGS ARE COMPLICATED

From the moment we are born, we reach out to the world, hungry to experience life with all of our senses. As newborn infants, we are drawn to the sweet, magnificently nutritious milk of our mothers, so from our very earliest days, we learn to associate the taste of "sweet" with love, nurturance, safety, and satiety. And this is a beautiful thing.

But then something happens. We grow up some, and something shifts. Our mother's milk is replaced by sugary factory-made cereals, milk with chocolate swirled into it, and prepackaged baked goods that have so much sugar in them that my teeth ache just thinking about them. What is offered to us as we grow may taste sweet, but nutritionally, it is the opposite of our mother's milk, so our naturally healthy desire for the taste of something sweet gets subverted by what we're offered in return. Our need for sweetness gets hijacked. It gets buried beneath mounds and mounds of sugar. And when this happens, our taste for sweet gets transformed into something other than a healthy craving; it becomes conditioned to point us in the wrong direction, away from the kind of sweetness we really need.

So a vicious cycle begins. We crave something. We crave something sweet. We respond to that craving by picking up whatever is in front of us, be it a candy bar, a sports drink, or the last slice of birthday cake in the office kitchen. We eat that "sweet" and we feel better — for a moment. But that moment doesn't last very long. Soon enough, we crash. And now we've got all sorts of bad things going on and we have to expend a lot of energy and effort to recover. When the craving inevitably returns, now it's stronger, even more insistent than it was before. We find ourselves giving in to that craving by eating something that is super sugary and nutritionally empty. We continue on with this cycle until we wake up one day and realize that we're fat, tired, and feel like crap.

This is when we panic. We decide that we will no longer give into our cravings at all. We'll starve those annoying, "bad" cravings. When our sugar craving hits again, now we try to ignore it. But it doesn't go away. It stays with us and makes us fidgety, or crabby, or tense. It keeps blaring, like a broken car alarm, telling us that we need something sweet. Frantically, we throw other things at it, such as salty, fatty, crunchy things. Now we've not only ignored our craving for sweet, we've activated another craving, this time for things that are salty and just as nutrient poor.

Now we are in dire straits and feeling

overwhelmed. Usually this is when we turn to the experts, the diet gurus, and we grab on to whatever diet plan is currently all the rage. Like a drowning person, we hold on for dear life, convinced that this diet, the one we've grabbed like a life preserver, is the one that will save us. And it might — at least in the short term. But chances are — and statistics show — that while most of us will lose weight initially, we will put it back on, and then some, over the long term. In other words, diets don't work. And I believe this is because most diets are, at least in part, about denial. They're about taking something, or many things, away. Most diets are generally about somehow working around your cravings, if not ignoring them outright.

Recently I came across some compelling research that shows that diets may not work simply because they are so mentally taxing. In other words, when we are on a diet, our minds are so busy keeping track of points, calories, a running tally of our food transgressions or our successes that we wear out our willpower and our ability to resist the siren call of cravings. In fact, psychologists have recently discovered that dieters actually self-generate cravings and lapse into fantasizing about forbidden foods much more frequently than nondieters. There it is, the unspoken Catch-22 of dieting: when you overthink what you eat, it can sabotage your efforts to eat more mindfully.

I propose that you will find your way into a healthy relationship with yourself — and your body — when you decide to stop dieting and instead listen to your cravings. Denial doesn't work. Deprivation doesn't work. But saying yes to your desires, to your real needs, does. Discovering what you most passionately hunger for is what will actually set you free.

Sounds straightforward and easy, right? But we all know by our own experience that identifying and honoring our deepest longings is incredibly challenging. We have been really well conditioned to hide our cravings — especially if they're for anything that's been deemed decadent or indulgent or rich. This is true in all of the really important aspects of our lives, especially those areas where *pleasure* is involved. I will touch upon all of these topics in this book, for sure, but for now, I'll stay with food, because feeling shamed or mistrusted or ostracized about our cravings happens most often when it comes to food.

We have been taught, first by our families, then by our society, and most aggressively by the diet industry and the manufactured-food-industrial complex, that our cravings are bad, that they're not to be trusted, and that if we indulge them, we will become at the very least fat or sick, or worse, unlovable and alone.

Of course, we are constantly being set up to fail; I mean, who among us has the unwavering ability to resist the mountains upon mountains of prepackaged junk food that block our access to the organic apples, which are usually tucked into an obscure corner of most chain grocery stores? Of course, we know intellectually that the apple is the better choice, but when we are in the grips of a craving, our "better judgment" tends to go out the window. When a craving hits us hard, our internal nutritional GPS gets all static-y and out of whack. Then we're easily led off track by the irresistible call of the easy, cheap, and convenient, which most of the time is the really unhealthy.

So, despite the sinking feeling that tries to warn us that we've gone off track, we all cave in and buy the cookies or the ice cream and momentarily satisfy our craving. But to what end? When we respond to a craving's call with a sense of urgency and emergency, we tend to overrespond and -indulge. If we take the opposite tack and decide not to respond at all, we risk triggering new, more urgent (and equally unhealthy) cravings. When we respond to our cravings in extreme ways (either too much or too little), we just get it wrong.

But our cravings aren't wrong. Usually it's just that we don't know how to best respond to them. I will help you learn the language of your cravings so you can honor them, and when you do, you will find yourself stepping into a state of radiant health and well-being.

HOW CRAVINGS WORK

I am asked all the time why, if cravings arise in us because we need something, do they lead us toward such unhealthy things? In other words, why do we crave chocolate or Cronuts instead of kale or carrots? If my body is nutritionally in need, why am I drawn to foods that are so nutritionally empty?

The answer is actually somewhat complex, and I will delve into the anatomy of a craving later in this chapter. But first, the short answer to this question makes a lot of sense: our brains respond with a level of intensity that matches the potency of the stimulation they receive. In other words, if you put a plate of chocolate-covered pretzels in front of a hungry person, her brain will light up like a Christmas tree because the stimulus in front of her — the attractive cocktail of sweet, salty, and fatty combined — is so strong. If you place a bunch of carrots in front of the same person, her brain will react in a much more subdued way (I'd go so far as to say that she'll even *relax* in front of the carrots, and may even feel a sense of calm wash over her, rather than experience the hyped-up excitement the chocolate pretzels would bring on). How we react to cravings is actually a form of call and response that is hardwired into us, and researchers recently have made some interesting discoveries about the neuroscience of cravings and what happens in our brains when a craving hits.

CRAVINGS AND THE BRAIN

"Why is my brain trying to kill me?" Susan asked, her head hanging glumly. We were in a café, having a cup of tea, and my brand-new client was sharing how frustrated, defeated, and hopeless she felt. She had been trying for almost half her life to lose a significant amount of weight that varied between 40 and 120 pounds. Now she felt stuck at nearly a hundred pounds over her desired weight and she didn't know why.

But she was on to something with this question, and I nodded in sympathy and agreement.

Susan is a classic sugar and fat craver. Whenever she feels any stress in her life, she is overwhelmed by an intense craving for something cold and sweet, so she turns time and again to her two boyfriends Ben and Jerry. "I get home from work and feel stressed out, tired, and frustrated, so I open a pint of ice cream and just go at it," she said.

She told me she'd unwittingly supercharge her craving by adding salty pretzel sticks into the mix. "I actually thought that if I broke up the ice cream with some pretzels, I would be, I don't know, somehow minimizing the calorie damage."

Instead of mitigating the damage the ice cream bender was doing to Susan's health — and her morale — the pretzels just augmented the problem. Susan didn't know it, but she was inadvertently indulging in the perfect storm of tastes that when combined completely overwhelm the brain, causing it to lose all reason and sense of portion and control.

Scientists even have a name for this phenomenon — the "bliss point," which is the high the brain achieves when it receives the trifecta of sugar, salt, and fat. When these three substances are combined, something happens in the brain that short-circuits its ability to identify the high intensity of each substance taken separately. To get a sense of this, think of three small glass bowls laid out in front of you. In one bowl, there is regular white table salt. In the next, there is refined white sugar. In the third, there is fat. If someone were to ask you to eat all of whatever was in each dish, you would think they were crazy, because each of these substances alone is just too intense for more than a tiny taste. But whip them up with some other binding ingredients and some irresistible flavors (chocolate is the king flavor of craving, especially for women) and voilà! You now have a cookie that is so delicious and so bliss inducing it defies your brain to eat just one. When the big three — sugar, fat, and salt — are combined, all bets are off and our brain loses its ability to discern that it's ingesting a tasty ball of junk.

Big Food is my shorthand name for the food-industrial complex, which plies us at every turn with unhealthy but ingeniously highly engineered foods. It has teams of scientists who invent things like the melting factor of Cheetos — what food scientists call the "vanishing caloric density" — a quality that tricks your brain into thinking it hasn't ingested any calories. The sensations of pleasure these engineered foods can bring on will trigger the same kind of high — as far as our brain receptors are concerned — as the finest street drugs. Food engineering, the quest for that lethal "bliss point," is serious, serious business, and the more scientists understand how our brains respond to food substances, the more easily manipulated we all can be.

I mean, who in their right mind can object to chocolate-covered salted caramel, especially when it's swirled into rich ice cream or embedded in a dense, chewy cookie?

But do not despair. Because knowledge is power, and we can be just as smart as those fiendish minds that keep coming up with new craving-inducing flavor and texture combinations that we have to work to resist. The key is to know how your brain is going to respond when it is seduced by junk. When you know what's actually happening when the sweet tooth neuron is lit up, you can make a rational decision about what to do about it.

YOUR BRAIN ON FOOD

There is a very straightforward, biochemical reason why we love our fatty, savory, or sweet foods so much. These rich substances release opioids (which are as dreamy and druglike as they sound) into our bloodstream, and when these chemicals bind with the receptors in our brain, we experience an intense sensation of pleasure, maybe even get a little high. When we experience pleasure, a desire is met and we feel good. Though this happy sensation may only last for a short time (even just for the moments that we're actually ingesting something, such as a piece of sugary candy), the memory of that experience gets stored in our brain circuitry. The next time we see the source of that pleasure, a craving may be activated.

Interestingly, researchers have shown that we may crave the source of that pleasure "hit," even when it's well out of sight, because those of us who diet and deprive ourselves of certain foods can conjure up those forbidden treats, and just thinking about them can trigger a mighty craving. In other words, dieters can actually fantasize their way into full-blown cravings, just by equating the lack of something they perceive as being desirable or pleasurable. (For example, there's that almond tart, sitting behind the glass at the bakeshop around the corner, the one you've been thinking about for the past three days. Or there's that chocolate soufflé on the menu at the restaurant where you will be meeting your friend for dinner next week. Just thinking about that dessert makes your mouth water whenever you look at your date book and see the name of the restaurant that features it.) The power of suggestion is so potent that even just thinking about foods can trigger a craving. Late-night television advertisers know this.

Cravings affect not one but several key parts of the brain, making them very difficult to pin down. The *hippocampus,* which processes and sorts sensory data like smell, taste, and texture, stores this information as short- or long-term memory. The *insula,* which frames the brain, processes your physical status (whether you are hungry, thirsty, tired, or cold) and cues you about what you need socially. The *caudate nucleus* is the core of pleasure at the center of your brain, which controls the release of dopamine. This is the reward center of your brain that feels so well cared for when you eat something sweet and buttery and suddenly feel comforted. Dopamine is the "orgasm" hormone, the one that makes having sex so fantastic, taking drugs so risky, and overindulging in the wrong foods so easy.

STRESS AND CRAVING

We are most susceptible to our cravings when we are vulnerable and our willpower is depleted, and nothing makes us more vulnerable than stress. Being stressed is for many of us the normal state of affairs, given how complex our modern lives are. But constant, low-level stress isn't normal — or healthy — for your body or your body's ability to respond to its desires in a healthy fashion.

When we experience stress, our bodies release hormones that are particularly potent and that tend to saturate us with sensations of urgency and emergency. When these hormones (such as cortisol) are coursing through our bloodstream, it becomes extremely difficult to resist our cravings, as our brain quickly becomes depleted of willpower and tells us that it is only by fulfilling that craving that our stress will be alleviated. Of course, this isn't true on a practical level, but when you are in a state of discomfort, reason and patience tend to go out the window, and it becomes difficult to access our better judgment. Reducing or eliminating stress in your life is a prerequisite to actually being able to hear the wisdom in your cravings, and throughout this book I will address how to contend with stress from many different angles and with many different tools.

FOOD CRAVINGS AND WOMEN

Research indicates that we women are more susceptible to cravings than our guys. In fact, some studies put that ratio at ten to seven, which is significant. The reason we crave more, in terms of our neurophysiology, is explained by our biology: as the carriers of young, we are designed to eat for two. This also helps explain why our cravings really flare up as our menstrual cycle peaks; our hormonal surges trigger a signal of "need" in us, activating that ancient part of our brain that wants to stock up and fatten up for the leaner times. Our menstrual cycles also pull most of the body's glucose to our reproductive organs, taking the brain's favorite fuel away, leading to more food cravings. It's not uncommon for most women to see a weight gain of a few pounds around the height of their cycle, when their hormones are cresting and they have yet to shed the lining of their uterus. It's as though the primitive brain is saying, "Wait! We may need to nourish a tiny someone down there — let's hedge our bets!" Then, when menses comes, our brain relaxes again, getting its access to glucose back, sensing that the need to stock up has passed. It's an interesting cycle, this monthly ritual of fertility preparedness. And it has deeply fascinating, uniquely feminine, and exquisitely personal manifestations as cravings. I love learning from my clients what menstrual binge foods they rely on, what their bodies seem to call out for in anticipation of taking on another life.

Then, of course, there are the legendary cravings of pregnant women. Scientists suspect that these odd cravings are a result of the wild hormonal roller coaster we go on when we're growing another human being. And though ice cream and pickles may sound gross, it's definitely a combo that hits the big sugar, fat, and salt triad. So wanting this makes sense to me.

How Cravings Differ
from Hunger

Part of my work is helping my clients understand the difference between cravings, which are a plea from the brain for something pleasurable, and actual hunger, which is the body signaling that it needs nutritional support. The distinction between cravings and hunger is incredibly important, but it is often hard to grasp, because there is a great deal of overlap with the two and it takes some knowledge and patience to learn how to tease them apart.

Because of our very busy, very overfed lives, the true sensation of being hungry is often hard to identify, but it is not difficult to understand. Hunger is simply the body's way of telling you that it needs fuel. Where a craving signals that there is a need for a pleasurable experience, honest-to-God hunger pangs let us know that we need to replenish our energy reserves. Where a craving hits hard and fast and usually quite specifically ("I have to have that bag of kettle corn right now!"), hunger is a slow burn and can be put off and eventually accommodated with a vast array of food options. The challenge is to not mistake our cravings — or any of our other appetites — for true hunger.

Most of us know that a human being cannot live very long without water. But did you know that the average human could live for about a month without any food? That's because our bodies are designed to store energy as fat cells, as a hedge against famine. For early humans — and sadly, for too many people around the globe today — getting adequately fed was and is hard work. For our ancestors, it meant being fast, strong, and alert, and when a hunt was successful, they tended to eat like there was no tomorrow, because in all likelihood there wouldn't be — at least when it came to having access to fresh, nutritious food.

So being hungry was — and can be — a relatively normal state. Our bodies are designed to function, and function relatively well, even as our energy stores are being depleted. But there's a point when we need to eat, to feed that hunger, in order to function at our optimal best. Learning to eat to keep our body and mind feeling and looking as good as we want is the goal. Discover how to listen to your body, discovering where, for you, being "on the verge of hunger" is, will open you to a whole new relationship with food. It is my great hope that mastering how to honor your own unique appetites — for healthy pleasure, nutrition, rest, work, and play — will help you to embrace all of your deepest desires.

Think of cravings as being a trick of the mind. Hunger, on the other hand, really does originate in the body, but it's not as simple as food in/food out, like most people think. As with cravings, feelings of hunger are triggered by hormones, particularly the hormones insulin, which regulates sugar/energy metabolism, and ghrelin, which is produced in the stomach when the body senses a drop in various energy sources. Ghrelin is essentially the hunger hormone. These hormones (and of course many others) trigger certain urges in us, and if we understand how they work, we have a better chance of responding to them appropriately. For instance, scientists have discovered that the stomach releases small amounts of ghrelin on a regular basis, roughly every twenty minutes, and after getting four shots of ghrelin, we're likely to experience a sensation that we equate with being hungry. This sensation generally hits us approximately every ninety minutes or so. When our stomachs are even partially empty, they tend to "growl" as they process the remaining contents, but this doesn't indicate that we're hungry; on the contrary, it means there is still food being converted to energy down there! We know we're hungry when a glass of water doesn't perk us up or when some time has passed and the feeling that we need to eat has intensified (cravings tend to pass in about ten minutes, whereas we can be hungry for hours, even days). As our hunger deepens, when we experience mental sluggishness or actual light-headedness, when our blood sugar, or as I call it, "brain sugar," gets low enough, it becomes clear to us that we need to stop and eat.

If you have issues with your insulin production and uptake, you may be overweight yet chronically hungry, much like my client Sarah. One of the challenges she and so many of us face is the fact that our body may be signaling hunger when in fact it is not hungry. Instead, it just might not be able to access the nutritional energy that is already stored in its cells.

But not eating is not the way to address this — at all. When your brain runs out of glucose, your willpower runs out. In short, your "brain sugar" levels need to be constant to keep your willpower strong. Feeling constantly deprived and stressed leads to calorie binges so the brain can get the fuel it needs. I know firsthand how resisting cravings or ignoring hunger can actually *sabotage* our weight-loss efforts. In my case, when I made radical changes to the way I ate because I was desperate to feel better, I learned, much to my surprise, that losing excess weight was a welcome by-product of changing my food choices.

Eating regularly, joyfully, and mindfully is the only way we can transform our bodies.

It is the only way we can live in harmony with our cravings and get in touch with what we truly hunger for.

REMEMBERING WHAT WE EAT

The great French writer Marcel Proust was onto something when he wrote so eloquently about the heady power of a small cake:

> I raised to my lips a spoonful of the tea in which I had soaked a morsel of the cake. No sooner had the warm liquid mixed with the crumbs touched my palate than a shudder ran through me and I stopped, intent upon the extraordinary thing that was happening to me. An exquisite pleasure invaded my senses.

Whenever we eat something delicious, or dangerous, or memorable, several areas of our brain are activated, and these include the memory, reward, and pleasure areas.

Think about it: most of us have certain "go-to" foods that we turn to whenever we get sick. It may be chicken noodle soup, or a grilled cheese sandwich, ginger ale, or Mom's magic tea. Whatever it may be, it's usually something that our mom or dad made for us when we were young, so that food's perceived healing properties are all tied up with our feeling loved, cared for, and well fed.

The same phenomenon occurs if we eat something tainted and get food poisoning: most of us can remember exactly what we had and where we were when the symptoms hit. If we were sick enough, many of us can no longer eat that particular food.

Whether the experience is good or bad, we'll have an intense association with that food, sometimes many years after the fact, because of the powerful impact food has on our memory.

When we lapse into craving a particular food, however, something really interesting happens to our memory: it becomes blurred, or dulled, when it's overwhelmed with the sensations of bliss that eating that food causes. Think about when you are sitting in a darkened theater, eating that movie-house popcorn that has been doused in butter flavor and salt. By the end of a 120-minute show, there's a good chance that you'll have worked your way through hundreds and hundreds of empty calories — without even noticing that you've done so.

The same kind of food "amnesia" can strike when you've become comfortable in your late-night routine, which might consist of tidying up the kitchen and, just before you turn off the lights, pouring "just one more" glass of wine or reaching for the chocolate that you keep stashed where the kids won't find it. In the morning, chances are you won't recall this late-night snack.

Cravings — or more specifically, the filling of them — can dull our remembrance of foods past. And these memories are things that we need to reawaken if we're going to be able to change our eating habits for the better.

CHAPTER TWO:
HOW HABITS HAPPEN

We are what we repeatedly do.
Excellence, then, is not an act, but a habit.
— Aristotle

The link between our cravings and our habits has been deeply and intensely studied, especially by those who want to unravel the mysterious power of addictions, which are in the most simplistic terms habits that cause us harm. Addictions are cravings that run roughshod over our willpower and our ability to make healthy decisions. We cave in to those cravings and start to believe that we have no other options, no other choices, and we lose control to that habit. This is when habits become addictions and this is when we've turned over our will — and our power — to the craving impulse. In fact, one could argue that a true, full-blown addictive state is one in which the person suffering the addiction is no longer capable of making any choices at all.

Here is how cravings can become habits: it is generally understood that when we crave something, and we give in to that craving, at that moment a habit *may be* born. But this is not always so. Someone who picks up a crack pipe one time may not become a full-blown addict, but there are a lot of reasons — aside from that person's willpower — that may influence why. For instance, some things we crave are very difficult to get, or prohibitively expensive, or so out of synch with the tone and tempo of our daily lives that we just don't have the time or inclination to go after them.

Developing a habit, an addiction, takes some time. It means responding immediately when a craving hits, every time. Repetition and habits go hand in hand, and this is most dramatically illustrated by the habit of smoking, which is considered by many experts to be the most difficult habit of all to break. That's because nicotine, the substance in cigarettes that soothes and enlivens us, has a very short half-life: once the cigarette is stubbed out, nicotine is no longer active in our bodies. So a smoker reaches for another cigarette. Then another. Then another. If a smoker takes in a pack of cigarettes a day, a quantity that many smokers would say is moderate, that means *twenty* times a day he has satisfied his brain's plea for nicotine.

If you've ever been or have ever known a smoker, you know that the craving for nicotine exerts so much control over that person that she will structure her life around her cigarette "breaks." The year after college I was smoking up to a pack a day, and my breaks were a favorite way to step away from my desk and get outside. But these were no breaks at all; these were the actions of a person who was no longer making decisions about how she responded to a powerful craving. In fact, I'd abdicated all of my self-control to a substance, one that was extremely bad for me. I was addicted, and I used my addiction to buy myself a bonus hit of free time away from a job I hated; so I got a two-for-one, which made the addiction all the more attractive.

All of us are guilty of this, this mindless giving in, and we do it most often with food. Especially if we are unaware and unprepared when a craving hits.

One of the facts about habits that I find so fascinating is this: it's estimated that up to 40 percent of our daily actions are habits. This means that almost half of what we do every day, we do without much thought.

Okay, so we shuffle to the bathroom and brush and floss, and while we are busy with this task, we think about everything under the sun, except what we're actually doing. We're on autopilot. We don't need to think about it. And there are many, many times a day when we go into this kind of sleepwalking mode, such as when we stop our work to find some information on the Internet — then find that an hour (or more!) has passed without us knowing it. Or when we shuffle to the coffeemaker in the morning and down three cups without thinking about it. But think about how many of these habits we'd have to tally up to equal 40 percent of our day. And our habits are sticky: they like to link up with one another and create chains of habits. For instance, if we habitually take the same road home each night, this might help reinforce the habit of stopping at the drive-through for a large order of fries whenever we leave the office late, which, come to think of it, is always (another habit is born). Before we know it, the habit of driving home on the same road has led us to stop at that corner drive-through yet again for another dose of french fries after a stressful day at work. It's a little sobering, don't you think, when we really stop to look at how much we do with very little, if any, thought? And this begs the question: What else are we doing that we're not thinking about? How else are we spending our precious time operating without any awareness? As it turns out, a lot of that zoned-out time is spent around food.

MINDLESSNESS AND FOOD

Food is our fuel, our great comfort, the source of solace we turn to either by breaking bread with others or, most poignantly and profoundly, when we eat alone. The habits women develop around food offer perhaps the greatest window into our unexamined needs, wants, and desires. Part of the great joy of my work is helping women learn to move past the many mixed feelings they have about their private relationship with food. This is not easy to do. It takes support and it takes time. But when we learn to keep the anxiety, fear, and judgment that invariably come up at bay, when we are able to just stop . . . and look, we begin to move past the cravings, past the entrenched eating habits these cravings have created in us, and we start to get a glimpse of what we really desire.

I speak to many women who harbor a lot of shame about how they relate to food when they are by themselves. All of us are alone from time to time, sometimes for long stretches of our lives, and yet as a gender we tend to treat eating, nourishing ourselves, as an offhanded, almost tedious or slightly shameful task that we rush through when we are by ourselves.

For some reason, we tend to heap a lot of dishonor on our relationship with food, and this is most true when we eat alone. I find that addressing how we eat in private, which is where our most entrenched and unhelpful eating habits tend to bloom, is an incredibly important and often emotional process.

My client Patricia came to me with a strong desire to lose the twenty pounds that she'd kept on since having a child more than twenty years ago. After her divorce her daughter went away to college, leaving her alone in her Manhattan apartment. While Patricia was a brilliant manager in a large accounting firm, and had provided leadership to her teams for decades, she wasn't able to manage her own eating habits when she left the office and found herself home alone.

Her morning routine was always the same. She'd stop at a bodega near her office and grab a cup of coffee, "regular," which in New York lingo means with milk and sugar. Around 10 a.m., like clockwork, she would have a "healthy" bran muffin, which she'd also picked up at the bodega. This muffin was the size of a small loaf of bread and was packed with sugar and gluten (a hard-to-digest protein found in wheat), which she hadn't yet realized was part of what was causing her to feel so bloated. She usually worked through lunch or attended lunch meetings where she would choose a vegetarian pasta dish, salad, or something else "light."

During the afternoon, she worked like a fiend, then usually at around 4 p.m., again like clockwork, she'd open her desk drawer and extract her "secret" chocolate croissant, which she'd also bought in the morning. By now, she'd been sitting for at least three hours, and without even getting up, she'd wolf down the croissant in a desperate attempt to refuel her glucose stores and alleviate the "fog brain" brought on by the high concentration she gave to her work, coupled with complete inactivity. By 7 p.m., wired and tired, she would get home and collapse in front of the TV and order Chinese or Italian take-out.

Patricia told me that she hated her afternoon croissant habit as much as she loved it. She knew it was keeping the extra weight on, and she knew that it wasn't actually helping her exhaustion. But the sweetness of the chocolate and the taste of the soft, buttery pastry was the only thing she looked forward to every afternoon. Eating this brought her a sense of comfort. So every day, she bought a croissant and told herself that she might not eat it. And every day, she felt her attention slowly drawn to the little paper bag hidden in her desk and would start to think about how good eating that would make her feel. And every day she felt a little better, for a moment, after she had closed her office door and had eaten the croissant. But then, usually within fifteen minutes, she felt terrible. The sugar rush would die and then her mind would start playing what she called "the blame-and-shame game."

"Blame and shame is when my brain tells me I'm an idiot for eating another croissant and so I deserve to be fat because I'm such a weak loser," she said at one of our first meetings. I understood that her work life was hard and that she did the best she could, under the circumstances. But what was her home life like, I wondered. Did she like living alone? With downcast eyes, she answered this question: "No. I hate coming home to an empty apartment. It's so depressing." I then asked her if she had had the chocolate croissant habit when her daughter was still living at home. Turning her head thoughtfully to the windows looking out over Central Park, Patricia replied, "I'd have them every couple of weeks, but it didn't start to become a daily habit until after my daughter left home." I watched Patricia's face light up with awareness as she heard what she was saying. "So I've been eating chocolate croissants to make up for my daughter being gone?" Then her eyes welled up with tears. "I must really be lonely," she added. Then she confessed to having a late-night ice cream habit that she hadn't told me — or anyone else — about. Every night she would scoop out a quarter cup of chocolate ice cream, sit down on her couch, and eat it while she watched the late-night news. Then she would go to bed.

We talked about the feeling of loneliness and how it actually felt. Did it show up in her body? "I don't know where it sits in my body — I've never allowed myself to really feel it. That's what the croissant and ice cream are for — to distract me from it!" Patricia's eyes took on a clarity I hadn't seen before.

"Would you be willing to sit with the loneliness for one full day and just notice how you feel?" I asked. "Will you just keep

67

track of what it feels like to crave these things and then, instead of indulging the craving, write down what you feel in your body, and what thoughts are going through your mind? Will you try to put words to that loneliness for me? For you?" I had a hunch that once she allowed herself to feel the natural sensations of loneliness, she would then experience the truth: that being alone was hard and the foods she craved were her mind's best effort to help her stop feeling the pain.

The next day, Patricia emailed me. "I won't lie, Alex: last night was tough. I made it through my afternoon by taking a meeting outside my office so I wouldn't be sitting there alone with my croissant. I decided to go to a restaurant for dinner instead of getting take-out, and that helped a little, too. I took your advice and ordered dinner at the bar. While I was there alone, the bartenders were really nice, and we chatted a bit. But once I arrived home, the impulse to sit on the couch with my ice cream felt overwhelming! I took a hot shower and got into bed early, but I lay there wide awake for an hour — it was so frustrating! I just wanted to have my treat and watch the news, like I always do.

"I got up and made myself some of that

herbal tea you recommended," she continued, "and then I sat on the couch. I didn't want to sit at the kitchen table, which I barely use anymore, because it is too close to the ice cream! I can't believe I was so powerless over this food! I felt obsessed and kind of crazy. I sat there with my tea, which tasted pretty good, and just looked out the window at the city lights. The feelings of being overwhelmed just made me angry, and then I remembered you asked me to write all of this down. I began to write, and then I just found myself crying over my tea. At one point, I heard my brain call me a 'lonely loser' and I just wanted to escape any way I could. But instead, I just sat and felt it. It felt like an eternity, but the bad feelings were gone in a few minutes. By then, the ice cream just didn't matter anymore. What mattered was that I was alone. The crying made me tired, and so I went to bed. I woke up feeling a little raw this morning, but clearer, too. I'm going to try this again today. Try just feeling instead of reacting to every craving that comes my way."

After a couple of months of discovering her true feelings, and her sensitivities to certain foods, like gluten and sugar, both of which made her cravings more intense, Patricia began to feel and look lighter. The extra weight started to fall away, and she began to take steps to create a life that felt full and connected and less lonely.

You may have heard the expression "You're only as sick as your secrets." With food, this is most certainly true. But, as Patricia learned, it's also true with our feelings; if we keep them locked up and hidden, even from ourselves, we are bound to be sick at heart. Isolation is a killer, and leaves us alone with our brains, which aren't always thinking straight. And when that happens, we're susceptible to making bad choices.

I can certainly relate to this. When I was in my twenties and working at a stressful corporate job that I wasn't passionate about, my eating habits reflected my disconnected desires. I got into the habit of tanking up on caffeine or sugar — preferably both at once — in order to keep my despair at bay. Without knowing what I was doing, I ate in a way that made me fat, made my skin break out, poisoned my gut, and triggered horrible, hot migraines that made it impossible for me to perform well at work.

One of my least helpful food habits during this time was my three o'clock chocolate break. Every day — and I mean every day,

Monday through Friday — I'd find myself slumped over at my desk, my neck and shoulders aching from sitting all bunched up in a bad chair at a desk that was parked in a dismal, poorly lit, and ventilation-deprived cubicle. By 3 p.m., I was always so depleted and droopy that I felt I couldn't do anything better for myself than eat chocolate. So I started to bring candy bars to work, and every day, the anticipation of "rewarding" myself with some chocolate at three would be lurking around the edges of my brain. Of course, eating the chocolate always worked — for a little while. But by the time I left work a couple of hours later, I always felt even worse than I had mid-afternoon. I continued this sad cycle until I saw that doctor who suggested I take a good look at how I was eating and what the cause and effect of those habits were. I actually tackled the three o'clock chocolate break first, and when I was able to let it go, it caused a wonderful domino effect when I realized I could break my bad food habits.

Here's what I did: for a week, I just took note of what I ate (Reese's Cups were a favorite), how I felt right after I ate it, and then how I felt one hour, then three hours later. One thing I began to notice is that having that much sugar coursing through my veins, without having any other nutrients in there to tone down its impact on my body, would make me crave even more sugar. I saw that I'd eat even more sugar after the three o'clock chocolate break — without realizing it. During this time, I was suffering from severe bloating and didn't yet know that my gut health was completely out of whack. I didn't know that the digestive tract goes wild when it's overwhelmed with sugar, causing the unbridled growth in certain yeasts and bacteria, thus causing bloating, gas, and bowel irregularities. The three o'clock chocolate break turned out to be the "gateway" behavior that was causing my gut health to get so out of whack. By eventually taking away this daily hit of sugar, I could see when I was reaching for sugar much more clearly, so I was able to control my intake of this drug (and yes, sugar is a drug) much more successfully.

After that first week of just becoming really aware of the cause and effect of this habit (I still ate the chocolate that first week), I decided to do it differently. I would take my chocolate break — but without the chocolate. I stopped loading up on candy bars over the weekend, so I arrived at work chocolate-free. I'd be lying if I didn't say that during those first few days, knowing that there wasn't a candy bar waiting for me stressed me out. When the 3 p.m. slump hit, I got up and went to the office kitchen and had a tall, cool glass of water. Then I went to the restroom and washed my face and hands. When I went back to my desk, I did not die. Instead, I got back to work and I left that evening feeling a little headachy, but noticeably less tired.

The next day, when 3 p.m. came, I got up and decided that I'd go for a walk outside and take in the sun for a few minutes. I was amazed by how it felt to step out onto the sidewalk and to be surrounded by other people milling around (this was in midtown Manhattan) and to just let myself absorb the energy of the city at that hour. I took a walk around the block, and when I landed back at my desk just a few minutes later, I felt utterly refreshed. And encouraged.

The next day, at 3 p.m. sharp, I left my cubicle and spent a few minutes socializing with a colleague, and then the next day at three, I made a cup of green tea. I started bringing fresh vegetable juices or protein smoothies that I made at home. Each day, when I made a conscious choice to do something different at the chocolate hour, I began to feel excited about my ability to make healthy choices, to truly take care of myself. I started to feel less enslaved not just to chocolate, but to my job, my cubicle, and the dull routine of it all. I began to *believe* that I had much more control over important things, over my desires, my body — my habits — my health. I realized that by changing just one habit — just one — I was changing myself. In very good ways. I was on my way.

How Habits Are Transformed

We all know what happens on January 1. Every year, we wake up and come up with a long list of things we'd like to change about ourselves or about the way we live. If you are a modern woman and you work outside the home and have kids or pets or other people you take care of, here's what your list of New Year's resolutions may look like:

Lose weight (this is always at the top of the list).
Spend less money.
Spend more time with the kids, my significant other, or my parents.
Exercise more.
Sleep more.

This is a pretty rudimentary list and it can, and often does, go on and on (drink less; quit smoking; buy a house; sell a house; get married; get divorced, etc.). All of these goals are great, and very well intentioned, but the way we try to make these changes doesn't take into account how habits are formed and how they actually might be changed. And so year in and year out, most if not all of us fail to fulfill our resolutions. We try, we fail, so we give up, feeling lousier about ourselves than we did last year. Sigh.

One of the biggest myths about habits is the idea that they can somehow be broken. The idea of "breaking" anything, if you ask me, implies exerting a huge amount of energy, believing that a giant act of will, a single mental blow, might obliterate something that took weeks, months, or years to develop. But this kind of strong-arming rarely works. Quitting a habit cold turkey does work at times, and for extremely dangerous habits, this can be the best approach. But for subtler habits — the habits of daily life — there is a better, more effective way.

Instead of trying to break a habit, think about *transforming* a habit. Let's go back and look at my chocolate habit. I still took that chocolate break at 3 p.m. every day, but once I became aware of what all that daily chocolate was meant to be fixing, I was able to address the problem differently. Before I brought my attention to this habit, I thought I was having chocolate at three o'clock just because I love chocolate. When I took the chocolate out of the picture, I found out that what I needed was to step away from my unhealthy work environment, to move my limbs, and to refresh myself by both hydrating and socializing, even if that meant just a few quick words with a colleague in the kitchen. In other words, I had to get to the heart of the matter to get to what I really needed, and it wasn't all about the sugar. It also had to do with my unhealthy situation (my job) and injecting some healthy, fun activity into my day, even for just ten minutes.

A habit fills a need. It represents our best attempt to quiet a craving, to address a desire that's gone unmet. If we've responded to that craving by building a healthy habit, we will find ourselves feeling calm, energized, happy. If we've responded in less than healthy ways, well, we've usually got a list (sometimes a long one) of all the ways we feel less than okay. And so we've got some work to do.

The first step to transforming a habit is to know that the underlying craving will still be there, that your body, mind, or soul has been triggered by a need. And this is okay. Knowing this, you can relax a little and get curious about the craving. The challenge is to not react and instead to relate. To get to the bottom of that craving and to find out what your body/mind/soul is really asking for. Once you have a better handle on what the craving is really asking you for, then you can experiment with various ways to meet that craving, just as I did — and still do. Every day at 3 p.m., even though I no longer work in an office, I either pause and have a moment of gratitude that I'm engaged in doing something I love, or, if I need to, I take a healthy, craving-calming break of some kind, which can mean taking a brief, brisk walk, drinking a cup of tea, reaching out to a friend — there are so many healthy choices to make. And they work, every time.

Adjusting our habits requires a gentle, loving touch, not a sledgehammer. We need to get curious about what we have become habituated to, what our addictions may be. Take my friend Jessica, a single mother who finds herself alone and tired after long days of working and caring for her son. Once her little boy has gone to bed, she often finds herself drawn to the pantry in search of something crunchy and salty to snack on. Most nights she's able to get her hands on a bag of popcorn or tortilla chips, and she'll eat while mindlessly watching an hour of television before she goes to bed herself. For her, this is her alone time.

Over the years I've noticed that the craving for crunchy foods is often related to an unexpressed frustration and anger. The hard crunching and grinding provides a satisfying physical release of tension. When Jessica and I talked about it, I asked her if those chips were providing what she was really looking for. She realized that there were some nights when she just needed to hydrate, so choosing a glass of water or a soothing cup of nerve-calming chamomile tea might be a better choice. On other nights, she craved companionship or a nurturing conversation with a friend. On others, what she really needed was to just go to sleep. And yes, there was unexpressed anger around her previous relationship and family that weighed more heavily on her at night. By talking it over, Jessica was able to see that she didn't really need or even want those chips late at night. When she was able to identify what she really craved, even as that need shifted and changed, she saw that she could respond to that call for self-care in new and healthier ways. This might mean taking a warm bath, getting out her vibrator for some deeply healing physical release and self-pleasure, or forgoing television and reading a good book instead; calling an old friend and catching up; or eating an apple and getting her "crunch" fix delivered in a much healthier way. Now, when that quiet hour comes, she's curious and in control, instead of being a prisoner to her old habit of snacking on the same kind of junk food at the same time, in the same way, day after day.

WILLPOWER: OUR MOST PRECIOUS RESOURCE

I don't know about you, but for a long time, I thought willpower was something I couldn't master, some vast and mysterious force, something other people had figured out that was just beyond my reach. I tried to stretch outside myself and find a way to tap into it. I thought it was the only way I would be able to crush my cravings, vaporize all my bad habits, and tackle every challenge life threw at me without missing a beat. Oh, how wrong I was! And how much suffering I endured, simply because I did not understand what willpower is or how it works.

Willpower doesn't come from without — it develops within. It is a very powerful resource, for sure, but it's not unlimited. Because it's finite, and therefore precious, it's essential that we become super mindful about letting our supply of willpower be depleted or inadvertently leak from a thousand daily wounds to our mind and body. Once we understand that our willpower can be drained by stress, fatigue, temptation, or feeling overwhelmed, and we learn to protect it from these negative forces, we can actually turn our attention to growing our supply of it. To do this, we need to focus on ourselves, to listen deeply to our bodies, and to tune out the noise of the outside world. For women, this kind of gentle yet intense listening is difficult. That's because willpower springs from our most authentic self, the self that isn't desperately focused on pleasing others first. It's the divine energy that manifests as self-control, or, more important, as self-care. Tapping into our willpower requires two things that most women have a difficult time doing: trusting ourselves and believing in ourselves.

Self-trust, which is the ability to tune into and honor one's deepest desires, is something that terrifies a lot of women. Many of us are freaked out by the idea that we might actually know what is best for ourselves. Of course, there are piles of historical and cultural reasons why this is so, but what fascinates and moves me is how, when I sit down with a woman one on one, and the idea of self-trust comes up, often deeply buried emotions come up also. So I sit in honored silence as client after client shares their deep pain, their shame, their confusion, or their sense of loss. And what is at the heart of all of these feelings is often the embattled, neglected self. In my experience, asking a woman if she trusts herself, if she honestly takes her own good counsel and advice about what she needs, triggers an avalanche of honest, raw, and beautiful feelings. Once these feelings come up and out, the healing — and the trust in oneself to be able to transform habits — begins.

Our deepest self, the authentic, unique person we truly are, is often lost to us while we're busy scrambling around trying to fulfill other people's expectations of who we are supposed to be. We've become habituated to being so "other-focused" that we've lost our ability to really see and connect with ourselves. So first things first: we have to relearn how to honor ourselves. Once you begin to do this, then you'll be available to bring active awareness to that 40 percent of your day that is governed by unconsciously taken actions of habit. When you are free to examine your habits with a clear eye, you can tap into your desire to change them. The goal then is to replace unhealthy habits with what I call "heart habits" — actions that will demonstrably increase your well-being with a ripple effect of effortless benefits. When you design your habits so they're adding to your energy level, your mental clarity, and your physical comfort, you'll find that you will be able to fill the remaining 60 percent of your day with the best of yourself.

THE ANATOMY OF A HABIT

Habits, much like cravings, serve an incredibly important role: they give our overtaxed brains a much-needed rest, a chance to go on autopilot and coast a bit. In fact, our brains love this so much that they are built to hardwire habits into their circuitry. The structure of a habit is really very simple. Think of a closed loop, an electrical track. There's an impulse, the engine that activates a craving, and once that switch has been hit, a habit is set in motion. We then take an action in response to this cue, which will then lead us to a sense of fulfillment. Urge felt, action taken, need met. Impulse. Action. Satisfaction. Where we have a choice is at that middle place, the place of action.

The key to transforming a habit lies in what action we choose to take. If we let our awareness nod off (which is what habits are; they are pretty unconsciously executed), and a habit has become deeply entrenched (that electrical track can be laid down very deep, like the solid, old subway tracks that crisscross the tunnels beneath New York City), we tend to forget, or don't even realize, that we can make a new choice and take a new action instead of just rambling along that old, familiar track.

It's big news to my clients when they learn that they no longer have to step onto that habit train and go for the same old ride. Part of the power of habits lies in how idle our consciousness becomes around them. When we're operating in a state of habit, our brains "forget" that we even have willpower or choice, that we have any say at all in how an urge or craving gets met. And when we forget that we can make a new choice, we're weakening our trust in our ability to change.

It's time to get that trust back. It's time to transform self-limiting habits into self-honoring heart habits, to rewire those tracks in your brain so your body and soul are renewed with the vitality of new possibilities. When your habits become nurturing, you will begin to experience life with the kind of playful freedom — the passion — you are meant to enjoy. Think about it: if the 40 percent of your daily actions that you take without any conscious effort are health building, energizing, and joy filled, then the remaining 60 percent of our choices and actions will likely be positive, too. Good habits beget good habits, just as surely as bad habits beget bad.

Okay. So where to begin? I suggest you start with a "heart habit" that lies at the crux of your life and impacts many other actions in your day. My lifelong yoga practice has a positive impact on my energy, connection with other people in class, ability to focus, and time management. This heart habit is simply going to class and stretching. But the ripple effect has productive consequences throughout my life that I don't have to work so hard on achieving.

To discover your own heart habit, look for any habit that you know makes you feel "less than" — does something you do automatically each day make you feel less fit, less rested, less lovable? Start there. Start with a habit that blocks something fundamentally important to you. This can be a bad habit that needs to be dismantled urgently, such as quitting smoking, losing health-threatening weight, or buying and wearing a helmet when you bike to work. Or it can be more subtle, such as making small but big-impact changes, like having a glass of fresh water and lemon on first waking.

Take my client Rachel, who really wanted to lose weight and increase her energy. Rachel and I sat down and talked about her diet. I asked her what foods she most loved, and her face lit up when she started to talk about cheese, and specifically, her passion for pizza, a favorite of most New Yorkers. As we were talking, I noticed for the first time that Rachel had a bit of acne, which is a red flag for some dairy intolerance, so I asked her to tell me where in her diet there were other sources of dairy, aside from cheese, which was obvious to her. And so we made a list: there was some milk in her morning coffee, there was cream in the butter she used liberally when she cooked, there was a ton of it in the ice cream she'd treat herself to after a stressful day at work. Given that it would be too jarring to ask Rachel to give up pizza as a first step, I simply asked her to try to notice the seemingly small amounts of dairy that dotted her daily diet. To make it a game, even. I also encouraged her to shift her intake of creamy, fatty, savory foods to lunch and dinner only. This was important, because rather than ask her to cut these foods out wholesale, I encouraged her to just have them later on in the day.

When we met the next week, Rachel was really getting into looking at her dairy habit. She'd taken the time to notice where and when she used dairy and she began to articulate what she liked about it so much: it felt soothing; she loved the creamy texture; it was rich, satisfying. We talked about how she could get the same sensory satisfaction she got with dairy via more nutritious, less disruptive foods. I gave her a list of delicious, nondairy options that included humus, avocado sprinkled with a good, crunchy sea salt, pureed veggie soups drizzled with olive or truffle oil. And there were so many delicious options for nut butters: almond, cashew, peanut, and my favorite, coconut. Thinking about these nondairy sources of richness intrigued Rachel. All of a sudden she felt she had inspiring, fun options.

When we met again two weeks later, Rachel was ready to address the elephant in the room: her pizza habit. I listened while she rhapsodized about her favorite pies, about how much she loved being able to come out of a subway and walk into a pizza parlor and be hit with that warm, yeasty smell. And then . . . that first bite of a fresh, hot slice. Man, I was right there with her. But it was clear to us both that Rachel's pizza habit was not serving her. Fortunately, she was in luck, because New York has several really good nondairy pizzerias. They are rare, for sure, but they are out there. So Rachel didn't have to forgo her love of pizza wholesale at all; she just had to try making another choice. Just once. That's all she needed to do.

I got a call from her a few days later. She'd tried one of the nondairy pizzerias I'd recommended. "I liked it!" she said. This was great news. I then shared with her the names of some really decent frozen nondairy pizzas and suggested she buy one and put it in her freezer, but to only break into it "in case of emergency," which made her laugh. I also suggested that whenever she felt triggered for a slice, to ask her body if it would be satisfied with a bite of dairy-free dark chocolate instead. She did, and this, too, seemed to beautifully calm her craving for dairy.

Now Rachel had options, and she was choosing them with genuine curiosity and care. But transforming this heart habit wouldn't happen overnight. It took a good solid three to four weeks for Rachel to get a handle on her dairy habit. For instance, she'd finish a latte, then realize a few hours later that the coffee she'd had contained milk. At these moments of self-awareness, instead of sliding into a state of distrust of herself and spiraling downward, she just took note, without judgment. And then she moved on. Rachel really understood that transforming this habit was all about awakening her awareness, and that this practice would take time. Once she became aware, she began to know and trust that now she could make a new choice.

I met with Rachel a little more than a month after our first conversation about her dairy habit. When we sat down, I was immediately struck by how clear and radiant her skin was, how bright her eyes were. Rachel proudly told me that she'd been dairy-free for more than a week, and that she'd lost five pounds during the month that she'd spent exploring her love affair with cheese and dairy. It's important to note that the love wasn't gone, it was just transformed. Rachel still loved dairy, but she was now clear on the impact it had on her body and energy level, and now she just chose not to eat those foods as often as she had in the past. She'd been patient and gentle with

88

herself while she gave her body and mind the time they needed to come together and identify the craving. Then Rachel was able to choose how to satisfy and soothe that craving in new, healthier ways.

Choosing the habit you would like to transform first is an incredibly important, almost sacred decision, because it is one that will open up your sense of yourself as a vulnerable being. Taking on that first habit will feel a bit scary, but that's okay! When we're vulnerable, we are our most authentic, our most human. When we step into our vulnerability, which is when we avail ourselves to change, we are stepping into possibility. This is why transforming habits requires a gentle, loving, and patient approach. And it requires consciously tapping into our willpower and then using it to guide our next self-loving action, even when we're afraid.

When I first met Lacey, her chief complaint was that she wasn't sleeping well. When I asked her how she put herself to bed, she laughed. "It sounds like you're talking about a baby!" In fact, I was. When my son was a baby, I began to notice and intuit what he needed to get the most restful sleep possible. I took note of all of the evening rituals we'd engage in, and I noticed that he would have trouble falling asleep if we spent the time leading up to bedtime listening to music and dancing around. On the other hand, he'd nearly fall asleep still wrapped in a towel after a warm, soothing bath. Learning how to prepare my baby for a sweet, restful sleep helped bring awareness to my own issues with sleep, so I began to look at my own sleep habits and made adjustments to my own routine, too. Now it was Lacey's turn.

"What does the hour before lights-out look like for you?" I asked.

"Lights-out? Actually, I usually fall asleep with the lights on." Lacey was single and lived alone. She worked at a tough corporate job and would usually get home sometime after 7 p.m. Even though it was late, she'd still cook for herself and eat a full dinner, which usually included dessert. By 9 p.m., she was full and tired. So she'd watch a bit of reality television, then grab a handful of tabloid magazines and trudge off to bed. She'd fall asleep surrounded by celebrity gossip, with the lights on. Then she'd wake up, usually feeling bloated and always feeling underrested.

I wasn't surprised she felt like she wasn't getting a good night's sleep: How could she when she went to bed with a stomach full of undigested food, her head filled with the images of impossibly beautiful people with crazy, dramatic lives? I'm sure that on some level, her dream-mind wove these tabloid tales into her own inner drama, creating life-style comparisons that would only add to Lacey's doubts about her self-worth. Both of these facts would absolutely make her feel vulnerable. But what was challenging her sleep the most was the unconscious fears she had about living alone; these drove her to always fall asleep with the lights on.

The adjustments Lacey had to make were pretty simple. She needed to finish eating, including dessert, at least two full hours before bedtime, so her body had adequate time to begin the digestion process. She needed to give up watching reality TV, at least at night, and she had to ditch the toxic magazines, which make us unconsciously compare ourselves to the celebrities they feature (*At least I'm not going to rehab for the fourth time! How is it possible to have boobs that huge when she is so tiny and skinny?*). This kind of reading is a habit that never leads to enhanced self-trust. I cautioned her not to fill this "quiet" hour with another brain-disrupting activity, like screen time, and instead use this time to have a phone conversation with a loved one, or engage in a relaxing hobby, perhaps knitting. These activities, I told her, had to be done outside of the bedroom. The only activities she could engage in, once she was in bed, were masturbating and reading, though it had to be with a physical book and not a digital device. The light from e-readers can trick the brain into staying awake, making it hard to fall asleep. And she had to turn out the light before she went to sleep, because her brain needed true darkness in order to fall into the states it needed to rest and recharge. I understood how this last step in particular would compromise her sense of safety, so I suggested she get a nightlight and make sure it was plugged into the wall in her bedroom before bed.

Lacey was able to make all of the adjustments to her pre-bedtime routine in just a few days. Within two weeks, she was feeling more rested, more alert, and more energized than she had in years. She was elated to tell me that now, instead of dreading bedtime, she actually looked forward to it, and that she'd embraced that last hour of her day as an important time of self-nourishment and healthy ritual. I loved hearing this, because creating rituals that fulfill our desires totally sets my soul ablaze.

How Rituals Bring Us to Life

How did we wind up where each of us has our favorite go-to foods, those treats we reach for when life gets challenging? Why do we overindulge in foods we don't even necessarily enjoy, like Grandma Bushka's sugary sweet potatoes with marshmallows, which we gorge on every Thanksgiving? There's a lot of crossover between food cravings and eating rituals, and when these things become intertwined, we find ourselves in the land of food habits, both good and bad.

When I was a little girl growing up in a DIY organic home, the law of the land was veggies and fruits first, then, if you were lucky, sweets. My parents were really strict about keeping soda and junk food out of the house, and despite a normal teen rebellion phase where I became a world-class sugar junkie, this early training has largely served me well. That's because I actually crave the good stuff before the bad stuff now; not all the time, but usually. I credit my early family eating habits and rituals with my body and mind being inclined to defer to healthy choices first. But I only default to healthy if I actively listen to my body. The "if" in that last sentence is where we need to put our focus, and I will return to it time and again throughout this book. That's because I cannot overstate how crucial learning to listen to your body is, in order to really understand its appetites and its desires. And we need this deep understanding to be able to make healthy choices.

We all have eating habits that we inherited from our families of origin. I encourage my clients to look at that early training, especially when it comes to rituals around food, because family traits and styles of eating often influence how we eat now, in very profound ways.

For example, if you grew up in a family where you had three square meals a day, at set times of the day, chances are you are likely to experience a strong sensation that you equate with hunger at these specific times. If you are used to having lunch at noon on the dot, you will very likely experience what you think of as hunger at 12 p.m. every day. But the next time the clock strikes twelve, try this: just wait. Just stay where you are for a few minutes and check in with yourself.

Close your eyes, settle down, put one hand on your belly, and breathe. Get quiet and ask yourself what your body is truly asking for: What is comforting about this old habit? Is this when you would touch base with your mom? Was this the one meal a day when you got to have a glass of chocolate milk? Was this a time of stress because you had to eat, hungry or not? Did you feel hemmed in by how rigid this routine was? If you spend these few minutes with yourself, you may find that you are no longer thinking about lunch or food at all; instead, you may find yourself thinking about your life, your feelings, your mood, your needs.

Usually, this short break, this slight shift in routine, is enough to change your relationship with that twelve o'clock lunch bell. It's enough because it takes the ritual out of the realm of the automatic, the unconscious, the habitual, and makes it conscious. It's brought an aspect of mindfulness — the crucial awareness needed for changing any habit — to the table. By giving yourself this quiet moment of reflection, your body and mind can calm down and the physical and psychological expectations for gratification will be quieted. You may find after breathing and listening in to your craving that you feel a slight surge in energy, a renewed sense of focus, and you may want to stay at the task at hand (be it work, chores, or your late-morning yoga class). You need to trust this impulse and let this happen. It's okay to let yourself break with family tradition.

It's perfectly okay to allow yourself to modify the ritual. Lunch will, after all, wait.

On the other hand, if after those few minutes you determine that you are truly hungry, then you get to decide what you want to eat so you will feel the way you really want to feel. So instead of heading to the diner around the corner for a cheeseburger and fries, you may decide that what would really be more delicious and fulfilling at this moment is a yogurt with fresh fruit, or a glass of iced tea with mint, or a handful of salty nuts. In other words, you may need just a bite, and not a full-blown meal. And that's all right, too. What you've done by giving yourself the space to breathe into your body and feel what your body wants is open the opportunity to make a new choice.

One of the greatest lessons of this kind of minimalist experiment is the dawning ability to distinguish between true hunger and habit. You may begin to notice during those ten minutes that you really didn't think about food; instead, you thought more about why you always stop at this moment. Then it dawns on you: eating at this set time was more of a ritual than a response to actual hunger. You may decide that you'd rather work another hour, on this day at least, or finish what you were doing and then go for a walk. All sorts of possibilities may now open up and you may actually feel excited — and empowered — for the first time by the notion of lunch. The ritual, the habit, has been broken, or at least put on pause, and what rushes in to fill its place is possibility and choice. This is when the magic can happen.

CHAPTER THREE:
THE BRAIN-BODY CONNECTION

"I've always been fat." Lysa said this so matter-of-factly it startled me. We had been working together for a couple of months and were in my kitchen, cooking a delicious, spicy vegetarian Indian stew that I knew would satisfy her type of cravings and energy needs. She went on, "I take after my father, who is a pretty muscular, beefy guy." Then she laughed. "No wonder people always ask if my mother and I are truly related."

Lysa is the daughter of a tall, athletic Latino man. Her mother is a fragile-boned, willowy, blond white woman. Lysa clearly inherited the best of both of her parents; she is stunningly, drop-dead gorgeous. She's also a size sixteen.

"My size wasn't always a problem," she went on. When I was in high school and college and playing sports, it was more accepted. I was strong and competitive and it made me feel kinda sexy. A lot of guys thought I was pretty hot, too." She laughed and then looked wistful.

"But for my mother . . . it has always been a problem. She wanted me to be more like her — slender, elegant . . . Other." She thought for a moment. "It's not because she didn't love me — she does! It's because she knew that it would be hard for me, not being the size that everyone accepts."

The pressure Lysa felt at home and from society at large to be a certain size finally caught up with her when she got to college. There she began to binge and purge in an effort to slim down. She'd get down to a size ten or even an eight, then, feeling deprived and weak, she'd eat as though she were starving — which is exactly what her body was signaling to her — and she'd rapidly regain all the weight she'd made herself sick to lose. The cycle was brutally hard on her moods and her body. Since then, she's had terrible problems with balancing her blood sugar, which has led to issues with her hormones, depression, and lethargy. She called me when she'd finally had enough and was sick and tired of feeling so low and so heavy. She wanted desperately to reconnect with her strong, sexy, smart self.

Lysa is a gorgeous woman who is just entering her prime; she's in her early thirties, has a great but stressful job as a legal assistant, and despite feeling fat, she's out there dating, hoping to meet someone who, in her words, "will make a great husband and an even better father." She lights up when she talks about her dating adventures and she brought me into her life to help her feel fired up right here, right now, in the present moment.

While the stew we'd made together bubbled on the stove, Lysa and I sat down for a long, comfortable chat. I wanted to find out what she really thought about her body, what she saw when she was encouraged to see it through her own eyes and not the unforgiving lens of her past experiences.

So I asked her: "What do you love the most about your body?" This one simple question stumped and even embarrassed her.

"I honestly don't know . . ." Lysa was, for the first time that day, at a complete loss for words. I smiled and sipped my tea. We had all the time in the world.

Let's be honest about something here: it's much, much easier for all of us to live in our heads than to live in our bodies. As a culture, we prize analysis over intuition, data over sensory experience any day. That's why we love our "experts" so much, especially those who feel compelled to tell us that counting calories, or logging hours in the gym, or eating the latest food bar is the best way to take care of our bodies. And the more forcefully someone tells us "this is the way," the more compliant and obedient we tend to become. At least for a while. When we sign up for the expert of the moment's program — whether it be one designed to help us lose weight, train for a marathon, or build our business — we often check our own best instincts and fiercely feminine intelligence at the door.

Pile onto this blind reverence for expert advice the crazy media-manufactured expectations of what a woman's body is allegedly supposed to look like and we might as well just give up on ourselves now. It's no fun being constantly bombarded with images of size double-zero models, these slightly alien-looking women who've been airbrushed and Photoshopped into angular Barbie doll shapes that have absolutely no relationship to what women actually look like. The only thing this fantasy-body hype has done for us is to further alienate us from our own bodies, our own physical wisdom. We look at ourselves in the mirror and see that we are "wrong." Therefore, whatever needs arise out of this obviously damaged body must also be wrong. What we feel in our bodies is absolutely at odds with what is going into our media-saturated heads. And because of this, most women I know have a horrible, shame-based relationship with their own bodies.

Well, it's time for that to stop.

We've already explored somewhat the way the brain responds to some of the basic cues your body sends out that are related to hunger or cravings. But what about the messages your brain sends to your body about your physical appearance?

Is your brain telling your body the truth? Is it working to help you feel more at home and comfortable in your own skin? Or does it cling to the crazy, inhuman standards that are fed to it by the media or by the incessant voices of our overly critical mothers or our own self-loathing?

It's time to check in with yourself and get really honest about how well you know and love your own body — the body you are in right now. It's time to find out if your brain is supporting your body's desires as well as it can, and if it's not, it's time to change your mind and bring your brain and your body into healthy alignment. And the only way to do this is to connect them through your heart.

I "Heart" My Body

Our culture likes to divide things in two, to think in terms of "either/or," and nowhere is this more evident than in our concept of body and mind. We really do think of our brains as machines that are somehow separate from the very physical, chemical systems that make up our bodies. But the truth is that they're all connected; our brains and our bodies are intertwined, and they intersect and meet at the most important organ in our bodies: the heart.

Think about it; our hearts pump our blood, the fluid of life, into and through all of our major organs, including the brain. And of course metaphorically, our heart is the home of all of our deepest longings and desires. It's the place where love resides, including self-love. And because the heart is so central to our overall wellness, we need to explore it more often. That cool, gray afternoon in my Brooklyn kitchen was the day Lysa began to search her own heart, and understand her cravings' messages, in new and transformative ways.

The Intimacy of Body Image

Lysa's inability to spontaneously tell me something she loved about her very beautiful, lush, and curvy body was not unusual: most of my clients have great difficulty taking a good, honest, and impartial look at their own bodies. Flipping the body-image lens and learning to look at one's body from the inside out, instead of from the outside in, is a very personal, intimate, and frightening process, at least at first. It can also be extremely painful, since we've become habituated to listening to the negative voices that shout at us from all of the counterproductive, and largely false, images of women that we're bombarded with daily. Combine this with all of the subtle and not-so-subtle negative messages we've been ingesting our whole lives, often delivered by the people closest to us, and it's no wonder that we can't say anything nice about our own bodies.

Learning to love your body as it is, at this moment, is crucial to transforming your habits, strengthening your willpower, and curbing your unwanted cravings. It's also the gateway to true joy, passion, and freedom. Learning to love your body — or at the very least to truly accept it without judgment — takes patience and time, and it begins with listening to what we're telling ourselves about ourselves. What you hear may shock you.

QUIETING THE
BODY-CRITICAL MIND

Since my initial question ("What do you love about your body?") had Lysa stumped, I asked her a different question: "What don't you love about your amazing body?"

Lysa perked up — we all have a list of things we *don't* like about ourselves. "Well, I know my legs aren't supposed to be more muscular than a guy's . . ." Wait a minute! Who said that? The look of horror on my face made Lysa laugh. "You know, Alex! We're supposed to have crazy Barbie doll legs! And these are not those . . ." Now she was standing and looking down at herself. "I mean, these legs mean business!"

"What kind of business?" I asked.

Suddenly she blushed, "Well, if the guy I'm currently dating had his way . . ."

"So. He likes your legs?"

"He does."

"But what about you?"

She got quiet and serious. "My whole life I thought that having muscular, cut legs meant I wasn't feminine enough. But my legs have always been that way. That's why I excelled at sports."

"Do you know how lucky you are that you're so strong?" I asked.

Even though Lysa hadn't played organized sports in years, she had to admit how great and shapely her legs were.

"So . . . maybe I don't hate my legs?" She wasn't so certain now. "You know what? I guess I love my legs, especially my sassy, sexy thighs." I could tell she was saying this mostly to please me, but there was also a new light in her eyes.

It's amazing how automatically, how unconsciously, we learn to view our bodies negatively, to reject them without ever really looking at them. Lysa was having a serious aha moment there in my kitchen. She was in many ways taking a look at herself for the very first time. It was just a brief moment, but it was a transformational one. She was starting to see herself honestly.

"Kitchari is ready," I said then, rising and going to the stove and stirring the aromatic stew one more time. Then we sat down to enjoy a beautiful, healthy meal together.

GIVING YOUR BODY THE BENEFIT OF THE DOUBT

Here's a hard truth about what happens when we don't love our bodies: if we're busy picking ourselves apart, limb from limb, then we deplete our willpower and aren't available to take care of the rest of our lives. Think about it: when our brains are filled with negative self-talk, especially self-talk that pins us down by negating the real beauty and strength of the awesome feminine bodies we're born with, then there's no room left to take new, positive action or focus on the good stuff; our brains get too distracted, too weighed down to focus on creating a life of passion and joy.

Our brains run on the tracks we lay down for them, and if they're running on negative, self-hating, self-limiting tracks of habit, they will run and run and run in a loop that doesn't promote health, well-being, or joy.

When we define our own body as bad and wrong, we're most susceptible to the lure of "forbidden foods." When we talk harshly about a body part, over and over again, we leave ourselves emotionally vulnerable in unhealthy ways and we become easy marks for food-marketing geniuses, clever gym owners, and whatever forbidden food we've got tucked away somewhere.

I have client after client come to me, frustrated by how powerless they feel over their cravings, but they've never stopped to acknowledge that they've already given up on their own bodies, that they have already, in really essential ways, sold themselves out. And when you've given up on your body, it only makes sense that the heart and the mind will follow. You simply can't beat yourself into loving your body.

Wherever your body is right now is where it ought to be. It may be fifteen pounds over where you'd like it to be; it may be bloated, tired, sluggish, or in pain. Wherever that body of yours is, now is the time to decide you are going to love it and care for it. Once you make even a simple mental gesture toward body acceptance, you will begin to release yourself from all of the old mental baggage that has kept you feeling heavy and too tired to transform your habits to this point. It's time to enter into a dialogue with your body that is productive and health affirming, to gently yet firmly take the wheel and begin to steer yourself onto a new course. It's the only way.

WHY BULLYING YOURSELF DOESN'T WORK

All of us have an inner critic that just doesn't know when to shut up, and even worse, this harpy is often hissing at us in such a low whisper that we aren't even aware that she's tearing us to shreds (often, ironically, while we're on a treadmill or yoga mat, virtuously passing on dessert, or otherwise trying to be "good"). I refer to this internal critic as the "bitch brain," and I've spent a lot of time getting to know my own bitch brain and working hard to turn her into my brain's BFF. It takes vigilance and cognitive awareness to dismantle the negative monologue that runs through my head, to catch those messages that undermine all of my conscious efforts to feel good about my body. But this work must be done; otherwise, all of the brightest possibilities for radiant health stay out of my reach.

Want to find out what your bitch brain has to say to you? Here's a little test: simply head to the nearest department store, preferably in the off-season, and try on the sexiest bathing suit you can find. Chances are that this will unleash a torrent of negative thinking about your body, and if you listen to the self-talk, or more honestly the self-lashing, that ensues, you may decide that you'll never go to the beach again.

So get naked. And get real about your body. Maybe your belly will never be flat, not since you had children, but so what? Instead of telling yourself that you're a loser because you've got stretch marks, why not praise that body for producing healthy babies? So what if your build won't ever be featured on the cover of *Sports Illustrated*? Who besides you in your real life cares? I'm not trying to be cavalier here, or worse, to offer empty peppy slogans, but the fact is, comparing brings nothing but despairing, no matter what you look like. What matters is that you accept the body you have — the body you are in at this moment — and know that as long as it's supporting you while you move to create the life of your dreams, then it is nothing less than smoking hot.

If you can't go there, if you can't love your body — bumps, dimples, ripples, and all — then you've got to do the work of breaking the habit of negative body talk your brain is used to. You have to catch yourself betraying your own body, of selling yourself out, and to do this, I recommend you strive to:

- Write a list of ten things you love about your body, post it on the fridge, and read it every single day.
- Refrain from criticizing anyone's physique, including your own.
- Focus on how you feel, not on a number on a scale or a dress label.
- Enjoy what your body does well (dancing, having sex, playing a sport, etc.).

- Don't be intimidated by media-driven size/body-type discrimination. In fact, stop consuming that kind of media. Avoid all reality TV.
- Steer clear of diets or exercise programs that are rigid, strict, and based on deprivation.

We've got enough stacked against us without being against ourselves. That's why it's crucial to break the mental habits that keep us from making peace with our bodies.

When our energy is spent building or reinforcing self-sabotaging habits of mind, body, or spirit, we will remain slaves to our cravings. Shaming and hating your body undermines all of your best intentions and makes it impossible to enjoy eating, making love, or engaging in any activities you love. It dulls our creativity and limits the healthy brain power we need to succeed at work and at home. So you've got to fight for your right to love your body. It's the only way to be truly free.

WHAT'S YOUR TYPE?

I'm a big believer that identifying and understanding your body type is crucial to being able to establish the heart habits that are really going to support you and unleash

111

your passions. I'm a fan of any tool that helps you mindfully shed the routines and rituals that have been keeping you down. But I'm not a fan of the rudimentary (and, frankly, pretty rude) body types that we see in places like women's magazines. I'm just not comfortable encouraging any woman to compare herself to a piece of fruit (I don't know any women who look like an apple or pear) or a geometric shape (triangle, anyone?). These "body types" just further separate the body from the brain and promote a sense that our bodies are objects that can be easily categorized. They just completely miss the point.

That's why I fell in love with Ayurvedic principles of holistic health. Ayurveda, "the science of life," is an ancient Indian philosophy that honors and elevates the wellness of the individual, body and soul. It is a celebration, a powerful acknowledgment of how unique and valuable each of us is, a system that is intimate and universal at the same time. It is built around prevention and diet — food is viewed as medicine and essential to health and wellness, as are our habits. At the heart of this life-affirming system are the five master elements (fire, air, water, earth, and space), and these elements become manifest in three primary energies, or doshas. These life energies are all present in every one of us in varying amounts. These energies combine into three body and cravings types: written in Sansrit, they are called Vata, Pitta, and Kapha. The language of the doshas is so beautiful and poetic — and, to my mind, very wonderfully feminine. When the Vata is balanced, you will experience high vitality and deepened creativity; with balanced Pitta, you'll feel more content and your intellect will be sharpened; when your Kapha energy is in balance, you will express love and forgiveness more readily. The Ayurvedic system is built around the notion that you are born with a dominant dosha type, and this type informs not just your spirit, but your body, too, although as you age and change and evolve, your dosha energies will shift and change. Ayurveda acknowledges impermanence and how fleeting and fluid our existence is. It's imbued with such reverence for life that I've found it irresistible in how affirming and accepting it is of the human condition.

I first experienced the power of the three types when I attended an Ayurvedic workshop for women in New York at the beginning of my training. I remember being in a big, bright, warm room on a snowy day and the instructor asking each of us to identify which dosha best described us and then move to the side of the room to join up with others of our "type." I moved over to be with the other Vatas, and then the instructor asked us all to step into the center of the room and form a circle. I looked over at the Pittas on one side of me and the Kaphas on the other, and I remember how true I realized the doshas to be. Here I was, in the midst of the Vatas, and my group was noticeably taller than the rest — and way more chatty. Our segment of the circle kept buckling and moving because none of us could stand still (too excitable!) for too long. Next to us, the Pittas, who were of medium build, were talking but not too loudly, and not with the same kind of rah-rah energy coming from my group. On the other side of us, the Kaphas looked ready to take on the world; this group of women were the most curvy, the most steady, the most strong. And they were the quietest among us. But taken as a whole, the energy that this circle gave off was crazy! It was so positive and vibrant and female. We stayed in that circle for some time, just resonating with all of that good energy. When I left that workshop, I felt like I had insight into who I am and what makes me tick in new, extremely helpful ways. Since then, I've incorporated the inclusive, body-positive teaching of Ayurveda into my own coaching practice.

Making your doshas happy will make you happy.
— Deepak Chopra

Honoring your cravings honors you.
— Alexandra Jamieson

As my work as a holistic health counselor has evolved and deepened, I have modified the concept of the doshas in ways that I believe more directly speak to my clients. I use my own version of the three great energy paradigms to help my clients become more comfortable with their own body type. I refer to them as the Featherweight (Vata), Firebrand (Pitta), and Earth Mamma (Kapha).

THE FEATHERWEIGHT, FIREBRAND, AND EARTH MAMMA

I know it sounds like I'm going to crack a joke about how these three body types walked into a bar, but truly, these archetypes articulate the very best of our feminine essence, and knowing how these energies inform our bodies, our personalities, and our temperaments can help guide us to better understand our cravings and habits.

The first, the Featherweight, is a woman who would lift off and fly if she could. Her thoughts and even her body tend to be airy, wispy, and easily buffeted about by the changing winds of the world around her. I know, because I'm a classic Featherweight, being tall and long-limbed and pretty fine-boned. We are creative and love to engage both body and soul in things that move us, be it dance, hot sex, or writing. Carrying extra weight, as a rule, isn't a problem for us because we're usually too distracted to focus on food. But eating on the fly can be problematic, too; when we put eating low on our priority list, we run the risk of neglecting our bodies nutritionally. Also, since we tend toward being cold — cold hands, cold feet — we need to stay bundled up and make sure that we're adequately fueling up. We also need to make sure we hydrate to keep our hummingbird engines running smoothly so we can keep flitting around. Featherweights can find balance in meditation, rest, and solitude.

Firebrands are the middleweights. Women of this type tend to be well proportioned and of medium build with medium bone structure. Their physical energy may manifest itself as high body confidence (Firebrands can wear anything and look great), and general good health. Firebrands tend to be athletic, entrepreneurial, authoritative, confident. They're good in groups and enjoy taking the lead. Their minds are quick but not flighty. They enjoy good food and feel best when they eat three balanced meals a day. The middle way works great for Firebrands; if they get too "hot" they may lose their cool, crave and indulge in too much alcohol or caffeine, or go all competitive on you. Easing up always supports a Firebrand.

Earth Mammas are the sturdiest, the strongest of the three types. They have the most energy, the most endurance, the most staying power. Earth Mammas, like my client Lysa, have curves in all the right places. Earth Mammas have to watch out about becoming too sedentary because all of that glorious Earth Mamma muscle needs to be put into play, to be put to good use. Earth Mammas need to move their bodies and they thrive best with long runs, hikes, or distance swims — anything that taps into the Earth Mamma's love for endurance will nourish her.

They're the deep ones; they think deeply and love deeply, often being more loyal than they ought to be, because they don't like change. Their internal furnaces tend to run hot, so they're often looking to cool down, with cooling treats like ice cream, for example. But they're prone to overeating and to getting sluggish and bogged down, so sometimes, on top of gaining weight, they'll also get a little depressed. Earth Mammas need to learn to slow down and savor their food, to know that there will always be enough and that they can relax around food and put more focus on tending to their emotional needs. This may mean pushing out of their comfort zone and becoming more social, more spontaneous than they're used to.

Lysa, my lovely Earth Mamma client, did just this. I got a call from her one day not too long ago, asking me if I'd be willing to come support her while she did her first-ever stand-up comedy routine at open-mic night at a local comedy club. "Are you kidding? Of course I'll be there!" I told her. I was blown away — Lysa's public persona was so understated, so shy. I couldn't wait to see her unleash some of the bawdy, beautiful sense of humor I'd been privileged to experience. Well, let me tell you: Lysa killed it. She was the only first-timer that night and she left all the regulars in the dust. She owned it! And the joy, the exuberant energy she gave off lit up that dark room.

Understanding and accepting our bodies is a nonnegotiable requirement for living an authentic and passionate life. Wishing that we had the body of someone else or that our bodies were somehow different doesn't serve us. (I was towering over all of my classmates — including the boys — even back in elementary school, and I remember having brief flashes of longing to be one of the petite girls, to not always be among the tallest in my grade.) But knowing what our basic type needs and craves and building heart habits to support that body type will bring us radiantly alive.

GETTING DOWN WITH GRANDMA FUN

A few months ago I invited a handful of my clients to come to New York to spend a weekend intensive with me. We spent the time talking about our habits — what was working, what wasn't — and how we could best support each other while we created the heart habits that would liberate each of us. We cooked and ate delicious foods, we wrote, and then we went out and got down and dirty.

Grandma Fun is the stage name of a woman in her midtwenties who is nobody's grandmother, but who discovered a love for burlesque. She's begun to build up quite a following in New York, and part of her work is to teach other women how to tap into and unleash their inner Dita Von Teese. She invited us to join her for a private class. There were six of us in a dance studio lined with mirrors and anchored by two stripper poles. When we first arrived, there was a lot of nervous banter, lots of reluctance to shed our coats, much bellyaching about how "fat" or "dorky" or "ungraceful" or whatever all of us were. Well, none of that mattered — at least not to Grandma Fun. She was all about us shedding our outer garments and our inhibitions.

So we got to work. Grandma Fun sat in front of us and told us her story. Here she was, a mild-mannered Earth Mamma with a dash of Firebrand, a woman who was putting off her dreams of dancing burlesque until she finally got into shape — and then her fiancé died in a fire. When she lost her love, she realized that life was too short to "wait for the weight loss" and that she had to begin acting the way she wanted to live now. In a teasing, relaxed way, she showed us some basic moves. Then she pulled on some elbow-length gloves, grabbed a feather boa, put on some music, and started to move. I don't think any of the rest of us blinked, let alone closed our mouths. She moved her body, smiled and showed off her sass, and held out rapt attention. Wow. She was *hot.*

"Now it's your turn," she said as she handed out boas and gloves.

One by one, weighed down by self-consciousness, we started to awkwardly sway and undulate, and as we did, Grandma Fun turned up the music and turned down the lights. The room became so intimate and so free that before you knew it, we were all moving with abandon. Grandma Fun coaxed each of us in turn, then brought us all together for some group moves. When she finally turned off the music and brought up the lights, we were all standing there, drenched in sweat, grinning broadly. What a blast! It was almost better than sex. When we went out into the New York City night, everything felt electric and alive. We said our good-byes with deep soul hugs and we agreed to wrap up our meeting over brunch the next day.

Checking in with my fellow "Grandmas" after the class was a revelation. I felt like I was with a new group of women; everyone was so vibrant, awake, alive. We ate, we laughed, and we basked in the glow of having stepped out of our comfort zones. Here we were, a group of women who represented the full spectrum of age, race, and body type, but we were all united that day feeling totally fierce and on fire — and fully present in our hot, hot bodies.

Discover your cravings type dosha and get more detailed information on how to eat and move for your type at: www.AlexandraJamieson.com/cravings quiz/

CHAPTER FOUR:
HOW TO BE IN YOUR BODY

There is more wisdom in your body than
in your deepest philosophy.
— Friedrich Nietzsche

I'm one of the lucky ones, and I know it. I
tend to be naturally thin, though, as you
know, there have been times in my life when
I haven't been thin at all. I've always been
the most comfortable in my own skin when
I'm in motion. Even today, as a busy working mom, I'm happiest when I get to cut
loose the way I did when I was still a free-
range kid. To fulfill this need, I decided that
I'd bike my son to school (weather permit-
ting, of course: Brooklyn can get hammered
with some crazy, over-the-top storms).
Though the logistics of getting my growing
boy strapped into his safety seat while not
forgetting part of our essential gear (helmets, keys, etc.) can be daunting, once
we're on the road, I always feel fine. In fact,

once I hit a certain stride, I feel great. I love parking right by the school door and delivering him to his day, knowing that we started it off with a pretty decent ride and some quality outdoor time together. Then, after drop-off, the ride home is a super thrill, because without him on board, I pretty much fly. I'm lucky that I get to do this. But more than that, this commute is keeping my body happy, helping it to stay in top form. I know, because this past fall, when the leaves fell and the temperatures dropped and I had to leave the daily bike ride to school behind, I immediately felt it in my cranky, crooked back. Alas, having my back seize up and cause me distress and discomfort isn't something new to me: it's a malady that I've been contending with for most of my life.

When I was twelve years old, I was diagnosed with a significant case of scoliosis, or curvature of the spine. Just like a character in a Judy Blume novel, I was fitted for an uncomfortable back brace that I was supposed to wear twenty-three hours a day. This contraption was made out of rock-hard plastic that was about an inch thick. It wrapped around my hips and torso in such a way that walking, sitting, and especially sleeping became not just awkward but painful. Wearing that thing made me so miserable, in fact, that in my sleep I'd unstrap myself and wake to find the brace on the floor beside my bed, my hips raw and sore from where it had rubbed me all day.

Of course, I couldn't wear regular clothes when I had that thing on: it protruded in odd places and nothing fit me. I couldn't wear jeans and short skirts, which were what all the other girls were wearing. I might as well have been wearing a straitjacket, because the brace made me walk with a stiff gait that only drew attention to the fact that my clothes (sweats and loose, ugly T-shirts, mostly) just sucked. This device was supposed to correct my "deformity," but all it did was make me feel . . . deformed.

It was awful.

But I was a dutiful kid and I took the doctor's warning to heart that if I didn't wear it for a full year, I would grow up bent over and misshapen. So I did my ever-loving best to stay locked into that awful thing day in and day out (except when I unconsciously freed myself in the middle of the night). But at the halfway mark, at almost exactly six months, I just couldn't do it anymore. So I stopped wearing it. I didn't make any announcement; one day I just woke up, put the brace in my closet, and got on with my day. No one seemed to notice, not even my mom.

Fortunately, part of my treatment included weekly chiropractic visits, and these seemed to really help. The chiropractor gave me a series of exercises to run through that spoke directly to whatever part of my back might be rebelling. These included doing muscle-building stretches and twists that would support my wildly growing spine. Plus, our health insurance covered medical massage, so my open-minded mom added these to my treatment mix, too.

I'll never forget my first massage therapist; she was a lovely, kind, middle-aged woman who wore her salt-and-pepper hair straight and long, which looked great with the caftanlike purple dresses she favored. She seemed to understand the unexpressed anguish I felt at being singled out and labeled as somehow being broken. She tended to my body with a loving, sensitive touch that not only eased the ache in my back, but soothed the ache in my young heart, too. With her, I learned to first acknowledge the muscular pain and tension that my scoliosis triggered, then relax into it while she gently, yet determinedly, coaxed the deep, tight knots out of my muscles. She worked on my body with such loving focus that I really experienced, for the first time, true body acceptance at her hands, and I'm certain the kind and healing imprint of her touch is still written on my body.

And then there was Lilias, the TV yoga guru. Every morning for many years my mom would arrange herself on our brown-and-orange shag carpet in front of the television set and she'd follow along while Lilias led her through a gentle, very exotic-seeming series of poses.

After I was diagnosed, I would join my mom on the floor, and even though I had pretty severe scoliosis, I was still young and super flexible. I'd bend with Lilias and just feel all this good energy moving through my spine. In those moments, even though I had no idea what "breathing into the stretch" meant or what "tilting your pelvis forward" was, I knew that my back felt better and cared for; it — and so I, too — felt good. I had no idea what *namaste* meant back then, but I knew that I liked how relaxed and happy my back felt after these yoga sessions. It wasn't until much later that I learned that *namaste,* a Hindu greeting, acknowledges the divine life force that is present in all of us, the healing, loving powers that are held within each one of us, especially when we take the time to care for our bodies by engaging in something as profoundly life supporting as yoga.

From these powerful practices and treatments, I learned that physical pain isn't necessarily a bad thing at all; it is often a clear message from your body telling you that you need to heal something. I began at age twelve to understand that the pattern of pain, relaxation, and release was essential to good health, and that breathing through all three of these phases — giving each of them that one key moment of direct acknowledgment and respect — was the way to health. At least it was for me, a girl on the cusp of womanhood whose skeleton was growing so fast, it was going a little haywire. And it is for me now, in my late thirties, as I continue to tap into the divine healing power of my own body so that I may rise, walk, and play every day.

DON'T OVERTHINK IT

Learning to quiet, or at least notice, your inner critic (that silly bitch brain again) is certainly a crucial step for relaxing into your body. But sometimes you just need to step out of your mind entirely and let your body do the work of calming itself.

If you've ever experienced any kind of physical trauma (wearing that back brace was certainly traumatic for me), then you know how hard it can be at times to simply relax. Think about how your neck and shoulders feel after sitting for a full day at a computer screen. How do they feel? Is your neck stiff? Are your shoulders relaxed? I'd guess that even now, just by reading this, you're drawing your attention to your neck and shoulders for the first time in a while and really noticing how they feel. I wouldn't be surprised to know that as you're reading this, you've relaxed your shoulders and aligned them some with your back and hips, and perhaps you're even releasing the tension in your neck by doing some simple side-to-side stretching. It's amazing what even the slightest bit of attention will do for your body, and how even minor physical adjustments can profoundly affect your sense of well-being. It's all about attention and awareness, without judgment, without insult.

Once you've quieted your mind, you become available to listen to your body. And once you begin to really listen, you'll find that your body will tell you what it needs to achieve health. If you're not picking up the clues that something is wrong, your body — and your brain — will find clever, and sometimes even scary, ways of getting your attention.

THE BODY KNOWS

All I knew was that I felt unsafe. For days, even weeks, I couldn't shake the feeling that danger lurked around every corner. And no matter how much I tried to talk myself out of this free-floating fear, it just didn't want to leave me. I'd experienced this kind of sensation before, where my "fight-or-flight" response would get triggered over something relatively mundane and the next thing you know, I'd either be in tears, under the covers, or, like now, unable to step onto a crowded subway, even though missing the train would make me late for a meeting. One night during this stressful time, I went to the theater with some close friends. My anxiety had been really high and I had, I realized, become a bit of a recluse. I figured that getting out and enjoying a great play might calm me down. I met my friends and we found our seats at the theater, but within minutes of the lights going down and the curtain going up, I was overcome with a feeling of dark foreboding, and I found it difficult to breathe. I felt so hemmed in all of a sudden that I feared I might jump up and scream, right in the middle of act one.

I didn't know it then, but I was having my first full-blown panic attack.

All I knew was that something was really wrong, so I got up out of my seat and crawled over my friends and to the aisle as quietly as I could. Then I nearly ran to the back of the theater, and by the time I got to the bathroom, I was drenched in a strange cold sweat. Thank God I knew what to do: using my index and middle finger, I gently but firmly tapped on the outside edge of my other hand. While I did this, I quietly said out loud, "Even though I feel so panicky and crazy I deeply and completely love and accept myself." I repeated this out loud as I continued tapping down the meridians of my body, on key pressure points: my temple, beside my eyes, under my eyes, below my nose, on my chin, and down to my sternum and heart. I did this slowly and deliberately, and almost immediately I felt my heart rate slow. Then the sweating stopped. I was finally able to catch my breath, too. The panic subsided. I took my time and splashed cool water on my face, fixed my hair, and then I was able to go back to my seat and actually watch and enjoy the rest of the play.

All of this took place in less than twenty minutes.

Over the next few weeks, I would still have

small flare-ups of panic, and of course they'd usually hit me when I was on a packed subway deep underground, traveling between Manhattan and Brooklyn. Every time even the mildest sense of panic would flare up, I would use the tapping technique and I would make it to my destination in one piece.

What I was practicing is called EFT (which stands for Emotional Freedom Technique), otherwise known as "tapping," which is a simple practice of calming your mind with strong, loving affirmations while tapping on key pressure points on your body. It's a brilliant combination of acupressure and spoken-word cognitive therapy. I'd known about EFT since my days in nutritional school and I had used it successfully over the years, but this was the first time I'd used it while I was in the midst of a panic attack. I was amazed and grateful that it worked so well.

EFT works to calm the part of the brain that is convinced there is a grave emergency at hand, and I can attest to how effective this very simple, soothing technique is. It's an incredibly gentle way of telling your mind to halt while you redirect your thoughts with those outrageously positive affirmations. It tells your body that it can ignore that urge to fight or flee long enough so you can regain some necessary alignment between your frightened body and your anxious mind. Simply, it calms the static in your mind so you can actually get back in your body. EFT is effective, costs nothing, has no side effects, and is self-administered. And to me, that's the definition of self-care in a nutshell.

Recently, a study done in Australia showed that EFT, or the practice of meridian tapping, as they call it there, even reduces food cravings. In the study, a group of nearly one hundred overweight and obese people were individually evaluated to determine the intensity of their food cravings and to rate which foods had the greatest power over them. They were also weighed and their BMIs (body mass indexes) were noted, as were general psychological profiles that outlined how each subject felt he or she dealt with temptation, stress, fatigue, and other factors. Then the group was divided in two.

The first of the two new groups was taught EFT immediately and was instructed to use this calming technique whenever a food craving arose. The other half of the test subjects, the control group, had to wait a full month before they were taught EFT, and during those first four weeks, their responses to food cravings were closely monitored.

After that initial month, those who were practicing EFT had significantly fewer food cravings compared to the control group. The EFT practitioners also reported a drop in the intensity of their cravings and many noted that the foods they felt they could least resist no longer had the same pull.

After one year, EFTers still reported fewer and less intense cravings, and their ability to hold off acting on their cravings was reflected in lower BMIs throughout the group. This indicated to researchers that EFT has a lasting impact, that it is a sustaining source of support for those grappling with overeating and cravings, and that it can be a very useful tool in supporting weight-loss efforts.

Looking back, I see that this period of extreme vulnerability, of fear, coincided with discovering that my then-husband was having an affair. We had a very young child, a baby, and not knowing if my family would stay intact, I felt very unsure and unsafe in the world.

I was fortunate that I had a very supportive network of people around me who were helping me get comfortable with the uncertainty that was rocking my world. I knew from my own work that if I could just refrain from being overcome with anxiety and fear that I would be able to weather the storm. And you know what? I did. I won't lie and tell you that it was emotionally easy or that the toll on my body wasn't great (it was). In fact, I had to scramble to learn about myself in deeper and more important ways than I've ever been called upon to do before or since.

The collapse of my marriage initially brought on a lot of pain and fear, but in the end, it brought me to a place of greater inner strength and awareness of what I wanted my life to look like. It gave me the opportunity to get really honest with myself in ways that I just hadn't ever been called on to be before. My marriage failing forced me to find myself, and I wouldn't trade that experience for anything in the world.

HOW I GOT BACK INTO MY BODY

After my marriage broke up, I often felt like I was having an out-of-body experience. My body seemed incapable of much sensation, so I dragged myself through my days without experiencing any physical pleasure at all. Plus, my scoliosis-induced back pain returned. I'd been carrying my son, who was now almost two years old, around in a sling that crossed my body, and my hips and spine were finally rebelling against this. On top of my back hurting, my lovely bitch brain was back, and she was determined to blame me for the end of my marriage, to make me feel like total shit about myself. I found myself inching toward depression, and I noticed that I was beginning to self-medicate with sugar, caffeine, TV, and complaining with my friends — all habits that would lead me nowhere I wanted to be. I knew enough to know that I had to do something to get out of my head. So I signed up for a Pilates class at the local YMCA.

Pilates is a type of physical conditioning that increases flexibility, builds muscle strength, and emphasizes spinal and pelvic alignment. Like yoga, Pilates calls for mindfulness and attention on the breath as well as movement. It's a system that promotes developing a strong core, or center, and it seemed well suited to my needs to get back in touch with my middle muscles, the part of my body I was totally estranged from. With the mat practice, which is what I like best, the resistance that builds muscle comes from your own body weight, so over time, a Pilates practice will not only keep your spine and the muscles that wrap around and support your core supple and flexible, it will help keep your bones dense and strong.

At first, I felt a little leery and distrustful of this new, subtle exercise, but fortunately I had a great teacher named Lauren who understood that most women brought a lot of emotional baggage into her studio with them. Lauren had a beautiful, serene presence, and she'd move through the class, tall and straight and confident, and speak to us with a firm but warm and loving voice. She was certainly on to me, because she would encourage me to move out of my head and to let my body do the work. So each time I laid down on that mat, I became more comfortable with how vulnerable I felt, how vulnerable I was. Over time, I was able to bring my anxiety and stress right into the Pilates studio with me. Then, as I followed Lauren's lead and moved out of my head and instead tuned into the wisdom and contours of my own body, I could feel all of those cares and worries literally rise up out of me and float away. I remember how emotional I'd become at first, because being there — showing up at all — was a sign that I was aware that I needed to take better care of myself. It felt terrifying to be beginning again, especially now as an adult and a mother.

The hardest part about being on that Pilates mat those first few weeks was really learning to trust my body again. I felt my ex-husband's rejection in every cell of my body, and it was showing up in my nagging back. Lauren encouraged me to close my eyes when she gave instructions, so I could locate within my body what she was asking it to do. It's amazing how understandable being asked to "wrap your abdominal muscles around your front torso like a corset" is when you can see it in your mind's eye and feel into the physical muscles she was talking about. I remember when I finally understood, in my body, when she asked us to lift our pelvic floor "as though it's an elevator rising."

I started to be able to connect to and appreciate separate groups of muscles: those that supported my belly, others that hugged the spine, and those that held the pelvic region. I started to feel alive again, in juicy, even sexy ways. Being on my back, on a Pilates mat, for an hour once or twice a week was making it possible for me to rise and walk more freely, more safely in the world. I was finally coming back to life. I began to

trust myself, to trust being in my body
again.

BREATHING INTO THE BODY

Another technique that is free, self-
administered, and utterly effective in calming the mind and getting grounded in your
body is the practice of conscious breathing.

Breathing is the ultimate habit; it is, aside
from the beating of our heart, the one thing
our bodies do without any effort on our
part. It's one of those unconscious mecha-
nisms that when made conscious becomes
miraculously healing and invigorating. I
mean, just try it. Stop right now and take a
deep, slow, deliberate breath in through
your nose and then, even more slowly, let it
out through your nose. Doesn't that feel
good? Whenever I do this, my eyes involun-
tarily close on the exhale and I feel immediately refreshed and refocused.

Breathing, aside from doing the key job of
bringing oxygen into our system, is the
number-one method of body detoxification.
In fact, it's estimated that we eliminate 70
percent of our waste via respiration. And
this is without any effort on our part! But
when we become mindful of our breathing,
magical, transformative things can happen,
including an increase in our ability to lose

weight. Studies have shown that practicing conscious breathing will also: strengthen your immune system; relieve pain; calm and balance your moods; realign your posture; stimulate and "massage" your vital organs; increase muscle mass; improve digestion and the absorption of nutrients into the bloodstream; and increase mental focus.

Clearly, the benefits to conscious breathing are many. And probably the most compelling is the sense of awareness and control conscious breathing imparts: it brings us immediately and gently, without fanfare or fuss, directly to the present moment.

Breathing with attention brings us right back into our bodies, which is where we need to be if we are going to live passionately and with purpose.

I first learned about the benefits of mindful breathing when I saw a biofeedback practitioner for a few weeks when I was in my late twenties. I was tormented over my fraught relationship with my mom back then and I really wanted to regain a sense of calm and reasonableness around it. The practitioner had me sit in a comfortable chair facing a computer screen. Then he placed a sensor on my index finger, which would measure my heart rate. He turned on the wide-screen TV in front of me and started an interactive video of a hot-air balloon floating across the horizon. The balloon's path was a visual representation of my heartbeat. The hot-air balloon bounced up and down, and would dip in and out of the screen. Knowing that the balloon was tracking the rate of my heart, I was able to see how agitated I was. Over the course of a few appointments I learned how to control my breathing and slow my heartbeat, so that the balloon would float across the screen serenely for minutes at a time. Learning how to control my body in that way taught me calming skills that I still use before speaking gigs, important conversations, and even riding the New York City subway.

QUIETING THE MIND

I've just got to put it right out there: I am not the best candidate to practice meditation. I'm too fidgety, to flappy, to eager to be up and at 'em. Sitting still is really, really hard for me (and of course there's my creaky back), and yet I discovered that I needed meditation in my life, just as much as I need clean water, fresh air, good food, and even better sex.

When we think of mediation, most of us call up the image of an emaciated white-turbaned guru, with a long, Rip Van Winkle beard, sitting cross-legged, eyes closed, on a craggy mountaintop somewhere very far away from wherever we are. I've always found this image kind of humorous, and even slightly "religious" in the sense that it suggests that we need to take ourselves out of the messy human game to find any kind of peace and enlightenment.

Well, what woman (or man, for that matter) can — or wants to — be so far from the action? Not many of us. Though when things get really, really hectic, I can appreciate the appeal of this kind of isolation.

During my divorce, when I found myself dogged by a low-grade but constant sense of anxiety, I did try to meditate in the stereotypical way of sitting on a cushion. I arranged myself just like the guru in front of me and there I sat silent and suffering, while my limbs went numb and my mind went berserk. I tried this form of practice several more times, and when I finally just acknowledged that this style of meditation wasn't working for me, I found others that did.

In particular, my brain seems to respond really well to guided, visual mediations. These are so easy for me because I can do them at my desk by simply calling up a video on YouTube or using a meditation app on my phone. There, I've got access to a fantastic array of mediations that can be anywhere from ten to sixty minutes long. All that's required of me is that I choose one, click on it, and then sit back and watch some beautiful, colorful images while a meditation teacher walks me to a place of calm and spaciousness. I find that I can meditate, too, when I walk or when I'm in a great yoga class, or even when I'm doing things like gardening, snowboarding, or cooking. It's all about reaching that state of relaxed flow, when the mind finally goes quiet and the body just takes over.

Meditation is a broad term, one that defies precise definition because it takes on different meanings in different contexts. Since there are literally dozens and dozens of known styles of meditation, I think of it in really basic terms: to meditate means to bring awareness to what is going on in your head. It's all about lifting the veil on what's flitting around in that mind of yours, seeing these feelings, sensations, and thoughts for what they are: fleeting. By acknowledging them through meditation, we release them and so we are able to return to our bodies.

Meditation has been very widely studied and it's known to reduce the cravings for some seriously addictive substances, such as tobacco. I would say that it works quite well for sugar addictions, too. And of course it helps with balancing our moods and improving concentration. It's all about awareness, and when we become aware, we regain some control over ourselves.

These are just a few techniques and practices that work really well to help us take advantage of that great, neutral gap of space and time and breath that exists between the mind and the body. I use all of them to help me stay present with myself so that I can open the door wide to cravings when they knock. Then, centered, I am able to invite them in, get to know them, and decide which ones are worthy of my time and attention.

SEEING BEYOND THE CRAVING

Another technique that helps us stay calm and present when the panic button of craving is hit is the art of visualization. We've all heard stories of people who imagined themselves with the perfect partner, or in their dream house — and then are told that because they were able to see their desire so clearly, they will now be able to achieve it.

There are whole industries built around this kind of visualization (have you ever made a "vision board" for yourself?) and there's a reason for it. Visualization works.

A 2011 study in the journal *Appetite* discovered that when an intense food craving strikes, an effective way to reduce the intensity of the craving is to visualize yourself engaged in a favorite activity that employs as many of your senses as possible. By thinking about how you want to feel, how you want to look, how you want to be in the world — in a very visual, sensually active way — you will actually begin to experience that kind of pleasure, without needing those sensations to be turned on for you by eating certain foods.

So, instead of automatically reaching for the afternoon bite of chocolate or late-night bowl of popcorn, take a short mental vacation. Try imagining yourself walking through a beautiful field of tall grass in the warm sunlight. Feel the breeze caressing your face and skin. Take a long, deep breath and smell the fresh grass and listen to the birds chattering in the trees. And while you're at it, imagine what you look like in this environment. Let yourself see yourself rested, relaxed, and wearing clothing (or not) that makes you feel really good about being in your skin. Trying this kind of meditation can evaporate many cravings. Then again, sometimes it's okay to just eat the chocolate, savor every bit of it, and just move on with your life, trusting that you give yourself what you need in every moment.

The *Appetite* study highlights what I've seen in hundreds of clients: when we start building in more pleasure, whether emotional, physical, or even imagined, cravings for food lose their power over us.

Whichever technique for calming your mind and restoring your sense of safety in your body appeals to you, remember: it's all about minding the gap. It's all about being strong enough to just *pause* when a craving hits. It's ironic, isn't it? Knowing that when we can just stop and do nothing — even for a brief moment — that's when we actually regain control.

Watch Alex's "EFT for Cravings" video and get mindfulness meditations to calm your mind and understand your cravings at:
www.AlexandraJamieson.com/WFDbonus

Chapter Five:
Detoxing to Discover
Who You Really Are

The body never lies.
— Martha Graham

Our bodies are our gardens to which our
wills are gardeners.
— William Shakespeare, *Othello*

The word "detox" is a complicated and
somewhat scary one. Before I came to
understand the great power in using detoxing as the cornerstone for breaking bad eating habits and establishing a healthy, relaxed
relationship with food, I had a pretty limited
understanding of what the word actually
means. Consequently, like a lot of people,
whenever I heard the word, my mind would
draw up a mental image of some poor soul
huddled in a dark corner sweaty and scared,
feeling really, really deprived. Even just
hearing the word would fill me with a mild
sense of dread, a sense of being at risk of

somehow spinning out of control, as though if I were not careful, I, too, might find myself in that lonely, desperate place.

I was thinking about detoxing only as it relates to helping people unhook from serious, life-threatening addictions. And back in the day, before it became something of a badge of honor (at least in the celebrity world) to go through a formal period of detoxification, there was a lot of shame surrounding the idea of detoxing. People assumed that those who had to detox were flawed in some way, or that they suffered from a lack of willpower or they didn't have enough personal conviction. Detoxing was thought of as a choice of last resort, the hard-line option that had to be taken or a life might be lost. When I was young, this was certainly how I thought about it.

But then something miraculous happened to me when I was in my twenties: I found out that detoxing — of methodically freeing my body from the food substances that were causing it harm — actually made me feel the *opposite* of desperate and out of control. I learned, much to my great delight, that detoxing gave me back my power, gave me back my sense of self, and, most important, it gave me back my health. My own transformative experience with detoxing was so profound that it led me to my life's work.

What I discovered is that detoxing from certain foods, behaviors, and emotions gave me the space and freedom to establish a new, vastly improved relationship to food and my body. When I was no longer pinned down by foods that didn't nourish me, my zest for life returned and I was able, for the first time ever, to tap into my true desires and needs. As it turned out, being jacked up on sugar was not what I wanted. Being tired and sluggish because I was eating foods that brought me down wasn't what I wanted, either. What I wanted was to feel at home in my body and at ease around food. Detoxing is what brought me there.

I soon learned that detoxing is a major feature in many spiritual traditions. Almost every religion has a ceremony or fasting ritual, from Christian Lent, Muslim Ramadan, and Jewish Yom Kippur, to indigenous vision quests that add medicinal plants like peyote and ayahuasca to their rituals. Detoxing is a proven — and sacred — means of self-discovery and healing. In traditional Chinese medicine, detoxing is used to eliminate toxins and restore body-mind balance. For many cultures, a fast or detox is an annual spring rite, used to lighten up and release the heaviness gained after the long, dark winter. Detoxing is straight-up cleansing, an elimination of anything that may be harmful, and this includes letting go of foods that either weigh us down, inhibit our mobility, hinder our thinking, or in any other way keep us from feeling free and at ease.

BREAKING THROUGH:
THE GIFT OF DETOX

Using a mindful process of detoxification, especially where food is concerned, is anything but an option of last resort. On the contrary, I believe that anyone who has the self-esteem and the courage to consciously refrain from eating foods that they believe or suspect are not helping their bodies function optimally are the most powerful people on the planet. Detoxing is a lot like skydiving; it takes a leap of faith, a true belief in your ability to take care of yourself, and the courage to know that you can and will survive a short time (or, if you choose, long term) without certain foods or substances. Detoxing levels the playing field and allows your body to reset at a neutral, clear point so that when you do add foods back in, you are able to really experience how your body reacts to them. The goal, of course, is to eliminate foods that you have

150

identified as harmful for good, and to replace them with foods that will better support your long-term health.

But I want to be clear here: when I use the word "detox," I'm not talking about harshly banning certain things from your diet and I'm definitely not advocating engaging in any kind of deprivation. Detoxing is about consciously taking specific things out of your diet so that you can then precisely assess how you feel when your body is no longer reacting to that particular substance. Detoxing is simply a tool to use to get clarity about how various foods and substances make you feel. Detoxing allows you to strip away all that is nonessential so you can find out who you really are and what you are truly made of. This is such an important distinction that I think it is worth repeating: detoxing is about discovery, not deprivation. It's not about self-denial or self-abuse.

In fact, when you are doing it right, a detox will bring you closer to yourself, closer to what you really need and want, rather than pulling you further away from the good stuff. That's also why there is no detox diet that is right for everyone. The gift of detoxing is finding out for yourself how your body feels when it is freed from highly reactive food substances.

Detoxing is about clearing things up. It's about uncluttering your palate, your digestive system, your mind, and your heart. It's about peeling away the layers of "noise" that block you from being able to really hear what your body wants you to know about yourself; it's meant to allow you to tune into your most ardent, authentic desires. It's about stripping away the things that keep you stuck. Detoxing is, above all, about finding freedom, especially finding freedom with food.

DETOXING AS A SPIRITUAL EXPERIENCE

When I went through that life-changing detox in my twenties, not only did my body go through a profound transformation, but my psyche and soul were also radically altered in ways that are very difficult to describe. And, I suppose, that's inevitable, because once you lay down the crutches of things like caffeine, dairy, sugar, and alcohol, just to mention a few, your direct, personal contact with the world — with reality — is immediately heightened and brought into sharp, clear focus. You realize that you are a vulnerable being, alive and electric, in a vulnerable, ever-shifting world.

When you strip away the stimulants, you find that the world is quite stimulating enough. You find that you are far more alive than you had ever known before.

All of this may sound a little bit woo-woo and corny, but it's not. I remember waking up one day, in the beginning of my detox, feeling refreshed and alert in a way that I had never experienced before. Nothing in my external world had changed, yet everything within me had; I felt clearheaded and energized and eager to address my life. I felt ready to take purposeful action. I felt like I wanted to reach out and embrace life full-on, on so many different levels. And I've made a commitment to myself to strive to feel this way every day since. And that's why periodically eliminating specific foods — which I refer to as "detoxes" — has become an important part of my life.

When we let go of the food substances that we think we need, we come in direct contact with our feelings in ways that often, at first, may overwhelm us. And so I always prepare my clients for the release of deep emotions that usually occurs during a detox. I'll be honest: detox requires bravery because you're letting go of your snuggly food security blanket, and letting go of anything we've grown to rely on for comfort is difficult. But once you do let go, even just for a few days, it's as if the dam we've built and have hidden behind for so long comes tumbling down and the onrush of feelings that this unleashes can be super intense. It's important that we know this may be coming and that we surround ourselves with as much loving support as possible as we go through this deeply transformative emotional part of the detox process. But this is where the gold is; this is where you can release so much emotional baggage that has been weighing you down and keeping you from really living. Detoxing allows you to get to the heart of the matter, the psychological and emotional issues that have been clogging you up. Once you're there, you realize that you've been eating to keep these blocks locked up and now, without food holding them in, you can release them. This kind of profound purging builds incredible trust in your own body.

One of the feelings that may emerge when you begin to unhook yourself from foods that you've grown reliant on is fear. This is the big one, the tsunami of all feelings. There's nothing like fear when it comes to activating all of our self-doubting, self-hating, self-sabotaging ways. And there is a lot of fear in us and around us when it comes to our bodies. When we're standing, nutritionally naked, in front of our fears and doubts (when there is no sugar rush to hide behind, no caffeine jitters to mask that terror), we have to be willing to sit with the discomfort that fear brings and find our way through it. We have to be able to rely on ourselves — and not some artificial additive or sweetener — to see us through.

One of the biggest transformations that takes place in detoxing is releasing that fear and finding that what lies behind it is deep, reliable strength. This is, to my mind, the greatest gift detoxing gives us: finding the innate strength to take charge of our diets and well-being in super-powerful ways.

What I've come to realize is that fear is actually the harbinger of good things to come. Whenever I decide that I'm going to take the actions I need to in order to take better care of myself, whether that's by deciding to have that difficult conversation, or forgoing a glass of wine so I'll feel good instead of tired the next day, or holding off on eating any refined sugar until my friend's birthday celebration next month, I know I'm on the right track when a sensation I used to identify as fear kicks in. For me, this feeling is highlighted by a surge in adrenaline, a particular kind of tingling that courses through my body. I may find my voice shaking when I make that hard call to not indulge or I may feel a moment of resentment when my dinner companions clink their wineglasses in appreciation while I hoist my sparkling water, but always — absolutely without fail — I feel empowered and more fully alive when I've taken these powerful self-caring actions.

Detoxing allows us to build the foundational strength of self-regulation and feel beyond the immediate itch or craving, to see down the road so that we can live with planning and purpose and not simply reactively. Once we let the fear of what deep clarity means pass through us, we find that we're on much firmer ground and that our relationship to food is radically altered.

This is why I encourage you to approach any kind of detoxification as the noble act that it is. When you approach a detox with true self-respect, you will find that the detox takes on the qualities of a great adventure and that there is deep pleasure to be had in this kind of experience. Healing yourself through detox expands your capacities for living and loving. There is nothing passive about deciding to detox; it is always a proactive choice, a conscious reaching out for something better. It may be motivated by a reaction; for example, the realization that you want to stop feeling bad about yourself because you eat too much candy and processed sugar. But that moment of reckoning, that moment of self-awareness when you decide to step into action, that's when you realize that you can do this and that by giving something up, you have taken a warrior's first step. Deciding to detox means you are committed to cleaning the slate, calming the mind and body, so your life can begin again.

APPROACH DETOX
WITH GENTLENESS

One of the aspects of the way I work that most surprises my clients is that I'm not a believer in the benefit of banishing any food from your diet for the sake of calorie restriction. Not only would that be silly, but it would be pretty overreaching on my part. I am not against any food per se, and I have no problems with people wanting to keep sugar, gluten, salt, or any other trigger foods in their diet. As I see it, the goal of detoxing is to experiment with foods that cause the most problems for most people and see how you feel with and without them. I see it more as a period of deep, personal experimentation, a chance for you to really get a specific handle on how certain foods make you feel.

If at the end of the designated detox time away from a particular food you decide you want to reintroduce it into your diet, then by all means you should. No one is going to scold you — especially not me. The whole objective of my work is to empower you about food so you can work with your cravings, to really understand them, so you can use food to feel the way you want to feel and live the life you really want to live. Detoxing is an essential tool to making healthy, lasting changes to the way you approach your life.

HOW DETOXING PROMPTS HEALING

The healing benefits of detoxing are so numerous that the topic merits a big fat book of its own. In fact, my first book, *The Great American Detox,* details the eight-week process I created to heal myself and Morgan Spurlock after *Super Size Me.* But for now, I just want to run through some of the most obvious and immediate health benefits that a simple detox will provide, even one that spans just a few short weeks.

When you take away the food substances that are known to mess with your metabolic systems — I have my own list of the "Toxic

Six": sugar (which includes alcohol and artificial sweeteners), caffeine, dairy, gluten, corn, and soy — you give your vital organs (which, of course, includes your heart and brain) a chance to rest and rejuvenate. We all know what can happen to your liver when you chronically tax it with too much alcohol: it becomes diseased and unable to do its job, which is to eliminate toxins from your system. So just think what giving your liver, your kidneys, your intestines, and your thyroid gland a break, even for just a month or so, will do for your overall health. You could, quite possibly, radically alter your health. I know I did the first time I detoxed and I have whenever I've detoxed since then. And I've seen hundreds of clients and friends do the same. Recently, a client who went through a six-week detox with me told me that she no longer had migraine head-aches — for the first time in twenty years. I've had people tell me that chronic heart-burn has abated, acne has cleared up, lifelong insomnia has vanished — the list of health benefits that detoxing can bring is dramatic and long.

Research scientists do know that a healthy, well-supported detox will also promote more efficient waste elimination. And we all know how transformative a proper poop can be! When your system is struggling to offload processed foods, salt, refined sugars, and countless additives and chemicals, it cannot do the more subtle and important work it was designed to do. Detoxing tends to correct problems like constipation and to improve kidney function, too, as refined, gummy foods like gluten-laden processed grains and dairy products are removed from your diet for a time.

Many clients have reported that detoxing has helped them:

• Jump-start weight loss: When your metabolic and hormonal systems are no longer ricocheting in response to wild fluctuations in insulin levels (which constantly signals your body that it needs to store fat), your body can naturally begin to shed unwanted weight.

• Strengthen their immune systems: Eliminating foods that cause inflammation and allergic reactions can give your immune system a chance to focus on more pressing matters. You may find, when you take toxic foods away, that you'll suffer fewer colds and infections because your body will have the energy and capacity for fighting off invaders. It makes perfect sense that cold and flu season descends upon us just as the sugar season begins. Cold and flu season really starts at Halloween, and grows in strength through the fall and winter as we indulge our way through the holiday season.

• Sharpen their mental focus: Getting out from under fog-inducing foods does the brain a world of good! When you lighten the burden on your body, you free your mind as well. And intuitively, you know this. You know you think differently after a glass of wine and a slice of chocolate cake than after a plate of quinoa, salmon, and broccoli. Clarity and focus stem from clean eating and avoiding foods that mess with your blood sugar regulation and your stress hormones. But that may be one of the reasons why detoxing from the Toxic Six hasn't been on your agenda until now. Because with clarity comes responsibility: when you see how your habits negatively affect your life, you have to take responsibility for this and decide that either you want to have a healthier relationship with food — or you don't. When you're foggy and spaced out most of the time, you can kind of float through life without really having to step up and take responsibility for yourself and whether you're bringing your best self to the world.

• Increase their overall energy: When you're not burdened by a sluggish metabolism and spiraling hormones, your energy levels can blossom. You may feel more inclined to want to move and stretch, which in turn will massage and activate your vital organs. We're designed to be active, to take action. And if you experience the energy surge that detoxing can bring, you'll feel more inspired to go after what you really want in life. That is, if you can manage the fear that this kind of responsibility can trigger; we can trick ourselves into thinking we're not powerful by allowing ourselves to feel subpar. Detoxing strips away these excuses.

• Swap good habits for bad: When you eliminate certain foods from your diet — even temporarily — you may be breaking a habit that you've had for a very long time. I find this to be especially true when people take caffeine out of their diet. They'll realize that after just a week or two, it may be the first time in years that they've gone for more than twenty-four hours without a cup of coffee or a soda or tea.

Unhooking yourself from caffeine can be one of the most liberating choices you may ever make, and I've found that breaking a habit like this empowers my clients to tackle other "bad" habits with a newfound sense of confidence and ability.

TRACY'S FIRST DETOX

When I first met Tracy, I thought she was a rock star; she dressed in fantastically stylish, hip clothes and she gave off an air of worldliness that was irresistible. But she'd called me because she wasn't finding the time to work on her writing and photography and she knew she needed to figure out what was blocking her. She asked me if I would walk her through a basic detox, where together we would look at the Toxic Six and see which of them might be causing her to feel so shut down. She was eager to start, because she was tired of feeling so lethargic, constipated, and bloated. All she needed was a notebook and some willingness and we were good to go. We planned on a straightforward six-week detox, where each week, we would eliminate another of the Toxic Six from Tracy's diet and look at how she felt without that particular food substance.

We began week one by cutting dairy from

her diet. Since Tracy's belly was bothering her (and she was prone to a bit of acne), I had a suspicion that she'd feel better right away, and she reported that she did. When we got together at the start of week two, her skin was noticeably improved and she told me that her belly had relaxed some. During week two, we eliminated sugars, both natural and artificial, from her diet. Tracy had eliminated alcohol from her diet years earlier, but she had substituted the sugar in booze for a whole host of other sweet treats. To help her stay away from candy, ice cream (I even wanted her to hold off on the coconut ice cream she'd just discovered), and baked goods (her weakness), I suggested she get a big bag of tangerines, lots of organic grapes, and raw almonds and keep them at hand at all times. This way, she'd be getting doses of sweetness, but without the corrosive side effects of sugar. I asked her to record how she felt without this substance during that week.

When we met again, at the start of week three, Tracy told me that she felt more energized and definitely more focused at the publishing company where she worked. She'd slipped a few times, but that was okay! She still had reduced her sugar intake for the week by about 80 percent. She'd also started taking regular walks past her favorite pet store in the evening, so that she'd be less tempted to binge. She'd buy an herbal tea from a café and watch the puppies in the window playing. I loved knowing that she'd added this coping skill, because she would need it for week three, when we'd tackle the biggie: caffeine.

"I don't think I will be able to survive without coffee," Tracy told me. I knew she would, but I also knew it wouldn't be easy. I encouraged her to take her time and cut back slowly, first by having half as much, then half that again over the course of a few days. By day four of week three, she was flying caffeine-free. By our next session, Tracy was a woman transformed: "It's crazy, Alex. I have more energy, but it's a calm energy — not that jittery, static caffeine buzz. I like it!" I loved hearing this. "But . . . I'm way more happy in my body, but way less happy at work."

So we talked about it. It seems Tracy was on a team that was designing a new Web site, and the people she worked with weren't giving her the credit she deserved. All the hard work she had put into the project was being minimized, as her greedy colleagues jockeyed to take credit for the work, since a bonus would be paid out once the Web site was launched. Tracy was disgusted and disheartened by this.

I wasn't surprised by this. Often, when we get out from under the side effects of toxic foods, and we're no longer hiding behind the veil of brain fog or under the weight of bodily discomfort, the truth of our lives emerges. This is what was happening for Tracy now.

By week four, Tracy was nervous, because she was suddenly craving sugar again, but she was able to see that this was a normal reaction to her needing to take some serious actions around her unhealthy work situation. "I get it, Alex, that I want to drug myself with sugar so I won't have to deal with work."

"Yes!" I almost shouted. She *was* getting it.

"But I can do this. I feel like this is worth it. Like *I'm* worth it." I reassured her that I would help her every step of the way.

During week four, Tracy eliminated gluten from her diet. This was a much easier transition than giving up either sugar or caffeine, because Tracy immediately experienced the benefit to her gut. For the first time in ages, she no longer felt bloated and her constipation went away. When I saw her again at the start of week five, she proudly did a runway strut in her favorite super-skinny jeans.

During week five, Tracy cut corn — and corn products — from her diet. I shared a list of alternative names for corn with her, and this appealed to her inner food detective and made identifying the hidden corn products that had been snuck into her diet fun.

Finally, during week six, Tracy eliminated soy, another ingredient that's added to many processed foods. This was the easiest of all to give up.

When we met again at the start of week seven — just a month and a half from the start of this detox journey — Tracy looked radiant. Her skin was clear and bright; her mood was high. She told me that she felt ready to finally address the situation at work.

"What do you think you might do?" I asked over a cup of peppermint tea — Tracy's new favorite.

"I'm not sure. But I'm going to begin by speaking up to my team, by telling them I'm not at all happy with how they've treated me."

This was a great place to start. I knew Tracy was going to begin to shed more than just the foods that weren't serving her, and that by learning to let go of the things that didn't honor her passions and her desires, she'd create space in her life for people and experiences that would.

The Emotional Benefits
of Detoxing

Tracy is a great example of how giving our bodies a break from toxic foods has the added benefit of loosening the emotional armor we've locked ourselves into. So many of my clients find that when they're mid-detox, lots of deep, unresolved emotions come up, and that now that they are no longer relying on foods to numb themselves out, they can process and release these deep feelings. Some of the feelings that may surface may date back to early childhood, and once they're released, you may find yourself on the cusp of a new stage of maturity, a new level of insight and wisdom. You'll have the opportunity to get to know yourself in deeper ways and to let go of old hurts, resentments, and regrets. It's a beautifully liberating time, and one that in the hustle and bustle of our daily lives we rarely get to experience.

The release of stuck, toxic emotions is another reason why having a kind and compassionate support team in place is so crucial when engaging in a detox. I know from my own experience that, like most things in life, it's much better not to do this alone. Detoxing with a group of like-minded people who also want to break some habits and find a more balanced relationship with food will buttress and fortify your own good efforts. And having a group or at least one other detox partner to mirror and validate your experience will greatly increase your chances for success.

I've heard from so many of my clients about the profound emotional break-throughs they experienced during and even long after they completed a detox. It's one of the benefits that keeps coming back to you once you've made the space for your emotional life to ripen and blossom. Here is one recent example of the kind of profound emotional change that can occur, thanks to detoxing.

GAIL'S BREAKTHROUGH

A strikingly attractive woman in her early forties pulled her brown hair back in a tight ponytail as she sat down in front of her computer screen. This was Gail, a client I was seeing for the first time. Once her features came into focus, our Skype chat began. Oh, I love how technology has allowed me to stay so deeply connected with wonderful women such as Gail who live all over the world. Gail was calling me from Israel, thousands of miles and a world away from me in Brooklyn. I had known her for a year, but this was the first time I was able to see the subtle shifts in her facial expressions as she brought me up to speed on her life.

Gail had joined one of my online group detox programs the year before, and she had kept in touch with me through Facebook. But she'd expressed her need to have a deeper connection, so here we were.

"Hello, Gail! Tell me what's new and good?" I had learned to focus on the positive, knowing that we are usually primed to focus on the old and shitty, and I took whatever opportunity I had to break that habit of focusing on what's wrong and learning to replace it with what is right.

Gail told me that a year in, she was still feeling really healthy and that her body felt strong. She had originally come to me when she found herself, a working mom with two kids under the age of ten, acting out when she was on the road for work. She'd get checked in, get to work, and then she'd find herself eating in her hotel room at night, when she was lonely and feeling stressed out. I remember her telling me that this

170

confused her, because she actually looked forward to the time alone, the time to recharge and get out from under her "mommy" duties, even if it was just for a night or two a month. So we addressed her feelings of loneliness and worked on strategies to help her take advantage of having a big bed to herself in a room with black-out curtains. I also helped her to go "off menu" with room service and order healthful, nutritious meals for herself. What a difference a year had made in the way she approached her on-the-road self-care.

"Alex! I've lost twenty pounds — can you believe it?" She was beaming. And yes, I could believe it. The same thing had happened to me, back in the day, when I had created my first detox. "The weight just came off so gradually, but you know what? I just didn't stress out about it; it just sort of happened, and I feel great about it. Even before I'd lost much weight, my colleagues started asking me if I was using something new on my skin because I looked so refreshed. One colleague even asked if I'd had some work done! It was pretty funny. But it's true: I look better, and I definitely have so much more energy. My body feels so much better and it just seems to work so much better. And my moods are more balanced, too. I used to become really emotional, really volatile, before my period, but now I barely notice a difference." Gail is an incredibly beautiful woman with deep, soulful brown eyes. I was entranced by her.

"I wanted to have this call with you to tell you that the toughest part of this last year has been, as you know, navigating my relationship with my mother. But I finally did it. I finally had that tough-love conversation with her that I've needed to have with her my whole life."

When Gail had first started a six-week detox program with me a year before this call, her mother had emerged as a surprisingly nonsupportive part of Gail's inner circle. This not only disappointed Gail, but it hurt her deeply. Her mother seemed determined to sabotage Gail's efforts at eliminating unhealthy foods from her diet, and she belittled her daughter's efforts to eat more cleanly. During the second week of the program, she'd asked me for some guidance about how to manage this. I told her I thought it might help if she asked her mother if she'd ever been happy in her own body. And if so, did she have a loving, supportive network of people around her who helped her to achieve her goals? Did she feel as though taking care of herself, body and soul, was a valuable way to use her resources?

These were the same questions I was asking my clients to ask themselves: Do you feel worthy to take the time and make the effort to feel as good as you possibly could?

This kind of deep self-inquiry cannot happen if we're hiding out behind food. And when we take the bold action of stepping out from behind the bad eating habits that have kept us stuck, we can, however unconsciously, seem threatening to those around us who don't feel entitled to make the same kind of changes.

It took Gail nearly a full year to have this tough heart-to-heart with her mother, including a few awkward false starts.

"The first time I tried to bring it up, we just fought — over what I have no idea. I felt like I couldn't find the right words, you know?"

Boy, did I know.

"But finally, when we were doing something far away from the kitchen, the kids — all of the stuff that defined us both — I just asked her point blank: Mom — do you love yourself?"

This one question led to a whole series of conversations between Gail and her mother about how different their lives were. Where

Gail's mother was valued for putting all of her energies into taking care of her husband and children as a stay-at-home mother, Gail was praised for being so successful in the workplace. Gail learned that her mother had struggled with how to love and support her daughter when her goal — to be a successful businesswoman who did not rely on a man for her income — was so at odds with how success was defined for Gail's mother's generation. "Self-love" was not in Gail's mother's vocabulary; it was for her, and her generation, taken as a sign of self-absorption, of not being devoted enough to those around you. At the end of a few honest, loving, yet often challenging talks, Gail had renewed respect for how selfless her mother had been and Gail's mother discovered that she really loved and admired how incredibly independent her daughter had become.

Gail felt this kind of emotional growth would not have happened had she not detoxified her diet first, and she wanted me to know this. I was incredibly moved by what she said.

"Taking dairy, gluten, sugar, and caffeine out of my diet gave me the chance to get in touch with my body, and it's wonderful that I've lost weight, regained my energy, and feel so present in my life as a result. But the big, miraculous gift has been being emotionally strong enough to finally forge an honest, loving bond with my mother. For that, I can never thank you enough."

Hearing this from Gail confirmed what I already know to be true: we shouldn't feel like we have to do this alone, and the more loving and supportive people we have around us are, the more successful we'll be in cleaning up our lives.

It's important to be clear about who is on your support team. Here's an exercise I like to give my clients. Write down the five people you spend the most time with. It could be family or coworkers, lovers or children. It may be less than five and that's okay. When I did this exercise right after my divorce, I only had two people on my list, and one of them was my two-year-old son.

Look at the list and ask yourself how happy, motivated, open, and supportive these people are. Do they feel good about themselves? Do they make you feel good about yourself? Next, honestly evaluate whether each of these people is helping you move forward in your self-discovery process or whether they're holding you back. Finally, tell yourself the truth: Are these the people you want to surround yourself with?

Are they really supporting you while you move toward fulfilling your desires?

This exercise isn't about breaking up with old friends, or not talking to those family members who happen to be less supportive than you'd like or need. This is about becoming conscious of the people in your life and whether or not they, like food, are nourishing you or weighing you down.

You may find that the people you spend the most time with don't really support you in the ways you need in order to move into a cleaner, more authentic way of living. In fact, you may discover that your current life is populated with people who are actually keeping you stuck or don't have the willingness to pursue their own deep desires. It may be time to do some housecleaning and bring in some people who will better support you as you go on this incredible journey.

Get more detox support, plans, and recipes at:
www.AlexandraJamieson.com/reboot/

Chapter Six:
Making Peace with Food

Your beliefs become your thoughts, your thoughts become your words, your words become your actions, your actions become your habits, your habits become your values, your values become your destiny.

— Gandhi

When we discover how to step beyond our habits, to really listen to what our cravings are saying, and we have finally decided that we want to live a life of agency, *a life of action,* the first thing we must do is make peace with food.

I hear a lot of groaning as I type this, because who among us doesn't have a gnarly, complicated relationship with food? Since Eve plucked that apple off the tree of knowledge, we've been a little freaked out by taking hold of our desires. We all know that it is the stuff of life, that eating is how we fuel our bodies, but this basic truth has been lost to us, hijacked and turned on its side by all the negative meaning that food has been buried under.

I'd say the number-one feeling that comes up for my clients, at least at first, when we start talking about food is fear. Yup. You heard right: we don't talk about what's delicious, what's satisfying, what's fun about food — and food should be all of those things to all of us — we talk about how food has a client feeling trapped, or sick, or stalled in her life.

Food, for far too many of us, has become the enemy. And no wonder: when we are constantly given the message that we're not supposed to enjoy our own bodies, how can we enjoy a meal? How can we love a food if it's become our secret, furtively gobbled source of comfort? Or a substitute for the partner we long for, that meaningful work we don't yet have, or all the other unmet desires and needs we've long neglected? When we are enslaved by our cravings, when we are food's prisoner, there is no way that we can enjoy that relationship. None. When we feel like we have no say about what our relationship to food is, then it loses all ability to please us.

If you've had a stressful day at the job and

you come home and pound a pint of ice cream, there is no way that the lettuce wilting in your crisper or the fruit you buy and eat only when you feel like you have to is going to look good to you. How could it, when in all likelihood you are riding a crazy sugar and fat high and hating yourself while it's wreaking havoc on your body?

At these moments, when we're lit up from caving into a craving, what is good for us has lost its appeal. We've fallen down the rabbit hole of habit, and the food that we really need — and, you will soon discover, the food that you really want — stays out of reach far above us, up there in the sunshine, where it wants to be savored and enjoyed. But we're down in that dank, dark place, too busy hating ourselves for yet again reaching for the wrong thing. It's a vicious cycle, this kind of habit-driven poor eating, and only we can break it.

It is not pretty. And we have all been there. So how do we find that sweet spot, the place on the teeter-totter where our relationship with food is pretty even-keeled and not wildly swinging from highs to lows? Of course, our relationship with food will go up and down, but these gentle ups and downs, the highs and lows — even these ought to feel good and not be too severe or traumatic. I mean, think about it. What's the best part of being on a seesaw? The ride. That's what it's all about. And that's what our relationship with food should be like, too.

And this is why I'm such a big believer in detoxing or cleansing or cleaning out your fridge (yup: even the year-old jar of Mrs. Richardson's killer fudge sauce is something that you need to let go of — at least for a time). First, you need to flush everything out of your system that has been holding you back. Once you've done that, then you can begin again. Once your system, your palate, and your brain are cleared, you can mindfully add back foods that you know will enhance your health and well-being. You can start a whole new relationship with food that will provide you with so much more than just the nutritional foundation you need to be strong, clearheaded, and in sync with your desires; it will also become a source of deep pleasure in your life. Count on it.

THE REVELATION OF THE GREEN APPLE

Every year since my divorce, I take a trip to Costa Rica with a group of like-minded souls who want to live more in alignment

180

with their desires. All I pack for this journey are my bathing suit and some really comfortable, easy clothes. I leave everything else behind, including my phone and my laptop. The purpose of this weeklong retreat is to detox from my everyday life, and so, at the heart of the detox is a complete break from all media. That means no texting, no TV, no music, no nothing.

The first year I went, it was pretty hard to relax. I was so twitchy it took me a few days just to settle in and be okay with me, myself, and I. Without anything but the lush, bright, and noisy jungle to distract me, I had no choice but to get comfortable in my own skin, get comfortable with what was going on in my overstressed brain and my broken heart. By the time that week was over, I was a new woman. I was sleeping better and I was calmer about everything in my life, including my relationship to food. In fact, my first trip to Costa Rica was when, as my friends love to point out, I realized that my severe judgments about how wrong it would be to eat meat were holding me back; they saw me fighting what my body was really craving, and I can see now that the struggle wasn't pretty.

Since then, the Costa Rica Retreat has become a great yearly reward I give to myself. For months beforehand, I schedule all of my commitments so that, come that winter week, I can take off alone and know that my household will run smoothly and my son will be taken care of without me; that my work is all up to date, and that I can slip out of sight for a full seven days and no one will even notice I'm gone. Believe me, I know, I am one lucky woman to be able to pull this off, and I'm grateful for all of the loving support I have around me that enables me to make this happen.

Every year I experience new insights about life and myself, and this year was no different. I had been sitting and just watching the jungle for several hours (you would be amazed what happens to your sense of time when you don't have to be anywhere and time is marked only by the rising and setting of the sun) and another one of my retreat-mates came out and sat in the rocking chair beside me. She took an apple from her pocket and a small knife and before she cut it, she asked, "Do you want some?" I've never liked green apples; I find them too tart and kind of tough and just not my thing, so I politely declined. "Are you sure?" she asked as she sliced the apple into quarters. She held one out to me. "Just give this a try." So I did. And . . . that green apple was the best thing I had ever eaten in my life!

I can't even describe to you what happened when that sliver of apple hit my tongue. I was overwhelmed with the most incredible sensation as my mouth exploded with a clean, crisp, perfectly sweet flavor that I had never experienced before. I turned to my companion and just started swooning and gushing over that apple. She started laughing and nodding her head in agreement as I went on and on, like a lunatic, about how freaking great that apple was. And let me tell you: at that moment, that bite of green apple was the best thing ever.

But here's the thing: I don't think I ever would have been able to taste that apple if I wasn't detoxed from all the noise of my normal life. I was only able to taste that simple piece of fruit, in all of its complex glory, because I was absolutely at peace and present. There were no distractions, just me and that slice of apple. It was one of those lucky moments when I felt so fully how beautiful eating is and how lucky we are to have access to so much healthy, delicious food.

Being in the Moment, One Bite at a Time

When you take away all of the overstimulation and noise, that is when you get to make peace with food. But you don't have to run to the jungle and do a full-on media detox, like I did, to get there. You just need to decide that you're going to back away from "noisy" foods — anything that's processed and comes in a box, a jar, or a microwavable container — and recommit yourself to discovering and eating foods that are untainted by chemicals and genetic and industrial modification and that are grown close to home. You know what I'm talking about. Real food. You need to decide that you are going to do your ever-loving best to eat only whole, fresh foods.

At first, redirecting your diet in this way may be hard. Transforming habits is sometimes a challenge. But remember, we are reshaping established actions, not denying you your life, which as you clean up your diet will begin to feel more naturally fluid and full. The transformation of old rituals, even the rituals we know are bad for us (that rewarding pull into the fast-food drive-through lane after a tough day, for example), can be hard, too, and very emotional. Plus, even though you are now pursuing an approach to food that is much more beneficial for your body, it's natural that taking away food substances that you've grown reliant on may cause some discomfort. (If you've ever been denied your morning coffee, you know exactly what I'm talking about.)

It takes a little time. And patience. And gentleness. But you will get there.

WHY FOOD CAN BE YOUR GREATEST SOURCE OF STABILITY

Discovering how to eat to support the rhythms of our bodies creates a state of flow within us, a state of easeful balance. When you eat a well-rounded diet (no restrictions!), you provide your body with the blend of nutrients it needs to function optimally. Eating a dynamically varied, robust array of food improves your mood, sharpens your mind, fortifies your immune system, resets your metabolism, fosters better sleep, improves muscle mass, strengthens your skeleton — the list goes on and on.

But here's the thing: a balanced diet is ever-changing. It's not a static thing. What you eat when you are eighteen and a standout on the track team is going to be very different from what you eat when you're thirty-five and pregnant with twins or sixty and launching your first business. Being able to go with the flow with your diet is what balance is all about. It's about riding the wave of your life.

ALIGNED EATING AND WEIGHT LOSS

I'm extremely prodiversity and antideprivation when it comes to the issue of diet and weight loss. Any extreme behavior — which is what most diets are — very well may prompt a dramatic weight loss. So many of these programs do, and hence their appeal. But research shows that not only does this weight not stay off for the long term, but that most dieters regain everything they lost and then some. That's because these food plans are too restrictive and limiting and so they are unsustainable over time.

Besides all of that, losing weight rapidly through calorie restriction is extremely destabilizing, and not just to your body, but to your willpower, mood, and spirit as well. When you've convinced your body that it is in a state of starvation and deprivation, rather than in the sustainable zone of pleasure, it needs to quickly deplete its energy stores (which is what releasing fat is) and sends out a message of panic that cannot be sustained over a long period.

We've got to *slow it down* when it comes to food; we need to spend more time thinking about it, shopping for it, preparing it, and eating it. We've got to be willing to enjoy it and find the pleasure it brings to our bodies. It's the only way to find peace and balance with it.

BEING FLEXIBLE WITH FOOD

As creatures of habit, our brains like to run on autopilot, and nowhere is this more evident than in the kitchen. Claire eats the same brand of sugary cereal every day, and she has for decades (even she will tell you this is the most committed relationship she's ever had). There is something about starting her day this way that puts Claire in touch with the most youthful, free-range aspect of her nature, and to her credit, she really mixes it up for the rest of the day to counterbalance that artificially jacked-up yet beloved breakfast. Since most of us aren't as slavishly devoted to one food as Claire is, most of us still do tend to keep our palates safe and our diets small — without even knowing it. It's because we're creatures of habit, and in order to really use food to find balance, you have to be willing to expand your palate and your pantry.

Here's an interesting experiment: try watching yourself as you go on your usual grocery run. If you are like most people, you grab a cart or basket and follow the same well-worn path through the store. You may start off in the produce section and mindlessly pick up a few bananas, maybe an apple or two, and then move on to the next aisle, and the next, until you find yourself feeling like your shopping is done. If you were to keep a log of what makes it into your basket and through the checkout line, you'd be amazed to see that over time, you are essentially buying the same few items over and over again.

Of course, this isn't entirely a bad thing. Our taste buds have been programmed to respond to certain tastes and sensations, and most of our choices offer us a reasonable mix of nutrition and comfort. But what if we could expand all that? What if we went into the grocery store and made a conscious choice to step off our usual path, to take the aisle less traveled? What if we started out on the other side of the store? What if we made the conscious decision to up our game and we went a bit rogue in terms of what we decided to buy, prepare, and eat?

Suddenly, grocery shopping seems like a pretty fun adventure, doesn't it? Now it's no longer just the mindless chore we have to do, like getting gas or taking out the trash, but a nutritional treasure hunt. Now it's about finding things that are both delicious and good for us.

This is a good place for me to stop and remind you that how you do anything is how you do everything: if you discover that you are shopping for and preparing the same foods over and over again, how else in your life are you stuck in a pattern that may be keeping you from reaching your true goals and desires? How else are your habits keeping you stuck? Maybe, along with revising your shopping list, it's time to rearrange the furniture, host a yard sale, start dating or masturbating, or take a vacation. Taking a look at what you do and how you do it (from how you eat to how you save money to how you make love) is what detoxing is all about. It's about shifting the status quo and making things better.

Once you've cleansed your palate and you've given your gut a chance to rest and heal, food gathering takes on a whole new level of meaning. Now you want to make sure that the foods you bring to your diet are ones that are going to enhance your well-being, not hamper it. For many of us this is a great opportunity to step out from under our habits and to approach food with a newfound sense of adventure and flexibility. We may find ourselves visiting a health-food store for the very first time, or driving in the rain to the farmer's market the next town over, or buying an Indian or Thai cookbook because we have discovered a new desire for more earthy, spicy, sensual food. Suddenly, deciding how best to feed ourselves is overflowing with delicious options and possibilities.

Deprivation? It doesn't even enter the picture. Nor does the sense that we're prisoners to our old, unsupportive cravings. With a cleansed palate comes a new start, a fresh chance to build better, more balanced habits. That is, if you are willing to remain honest with yourself about the foods that you now know cause you harm, and even more important, decide to honor and embrace the foods that will make you feel well.

Now there are no more excuses. There is no reason on earth why you can't become the adventurous, nutrition-savvy eater your body is craving you to be.

This is when food becomes fun. This is when we finally get to experience a little-known truth: food can make us happy — if we let it. It can become a foundational way for us to express self-love, to experience pleasure. It can become an incredibly powerful way for us to be radically self-caring. But we can't experience food this way if we're hiding out with it, abusing it, or otherwise giving it power over us. Food is meant to nourish and free us, not enslave us. But it's up to us to make sure our relationship with food is a healthy one, and in order to do this, we must stay flexible in our relationship with food.

THE NEW RULES OF EATING: THERE ARE NO RULES

We are living during a true renaissance when it comes to what we know about our bodies and nutrition, what we know about how food influences our health. We're aware of the importance of eating locally sourced, organic, and whole foods. Scientists are really beginning to understand how food affects brain functioning as well as gut health in ever more sophisticated, practical ways. We get it that sugar is a drug, and that overeating and undermoving are deadly habits. In short, we have more information about what we need in order to have a healthy relationship with food than we've ever had before, but still . . . we just don't trust ourselves. We still don't trust that we can find our own way with food.

And this is what keeps the diet industry alive and kicking. This belief that someone else knows better than we do; that some expert will tell us exactly what to eat, and if we're compliant and obedient, then we'll lose the weight, and then . . . what? What will we have discovered about ourselves and our very unique and personal relationship with food? How will we feed ourselves going forward? (This is an especially thorny question for those of us who have become reliant on the prepared foods or shakes sold by popular diet plans.) How will we find nutritional balance and health if there is no one there telling us what to do?

This is why diets fail. They don't teach you how to listen to your body. They don't empower you to trust your own excellent judgment about food. They don't, as a rule, teach you to discern which foods make you feel radiantly well as opposed to those that make you feel bloated and sluggish. That's because most diets are not a dialogue, they are rule books, and pretty bossy ones at that. It doesn't matter what the diet of the day is, many tell us to "eat this, not that," and if you don't, then you will fail. Oh, and be fat. And when you're fat, all sorts of bad things will happen. I mean, who responds well to that? What woman needs to be told it's "my way or the highway" when it comes to what's best for her body?

When we put someone else's rules of eating above what our bodies actually need, we further disassociate from ourselves and lose our ability to feel pleasure, which is actually our greatest ally in our journey to wholeness and sexy self-acceptance. Being flexible with food is the best way to be flexible with life. When we're open to new eating experiences, we are open to everything: new relationships, new sensations, new ways of being well in the world.

INTUITIVE EATING

By the time most clients contact me, they no longer have any idea what true hunger is. Oh, they know a lot about despair, deprivation, self-loathing, and shame. But very few, if any, have even the faintest idea of what it means to be truly hungry. That's because most of them have been spending their lives trying to outwit or outrun their desires and hungers by overeating, undereating, or seesawing between these two extremes.

When we are able to get in touch with our true hunger, it becomes a recognizable, clear-eyed inner counselor. When we honor it, hunger becomes our most intimate ally in our quest for true health, a source of support and advice that we can come to rely on to nourish us as our passions and our lives grow and evolve.

Our true hunger is the antithesis of the bitch brain; instead, it — she — is the voice of reason and reassurance that we've been needing, yet avoiding, our whole lives. Hunger is the voice of our purpose, our feminine power, our deepest desires. It's not a frantic, grasping, or whining voice. On the contrary, the true voice of hunger is patient, calm, and wise.

Getting to know and befriend your hunger is one of the most important relationships you will ever have in your life. It's like meeting your long-lost twin, the sister you always suspected you had who is just like you, but without all the self-judgment, self-sabotage, self-loathing. She is you on fire. And getting to know her and closing the divide between you is what this journey is all about. So you need to get to know her intimately. And you need to feed her in ways that will deeply support her.

The best way to do this is to eat intuitively. To eat to honor not just how you feel now, but how you wish to feel two hours from now, three days from now, one month from now, and so on.

The goal is to eat in order to live your life to its absolute fullest.

Let me give you an example of how this works. I have a client, Stephanie, who came to me several years ago because she wanted to lose fifty pounds. Until then, she had had one bad diet experience after another; she would follow the rules of whatever diet she was on, lose the weight, then when she had met her goal and the diet was done, she'd gain all the weight back — and then some. This story is so common it has become a cliché. Stephanie came to me because she had finally come to the conclusion that she needed to forget dieting and learn to eat for herself.

During our first meeting, I asked Stephanie what her goal was, and her response was "to lose this weight once and for all."

I took this in and then said it back to her differently: "I want to learn to eat food that nourishes me, makes me feel well, and lets me feel comfortable in my own body." I intentionally left the losing-weight language out of my take on Stephanie's stated goal, hoping that this might prompt her to look beyond the numbers on the scale, the numbers that had her transfixed and rather trapped by her inability to see her life beyond that scale on the floor of her tiny, cramped bathroom. By giving the numbers on the scale so much power, she left herself with nothing but lots of self-judgment and criticism. Stephanie heard what I said, but she wasn't quite sure if she could live with this more open-ended, fluid goal. But she agreed to try.

And so we began the process of Stephanie learning to hear her hunger, to identify what she needed and wanted for her body and for her life.

At first, this practice filled her with a lot of anxiety, because for the first time in her adult life, someone else wasn't telling her what to eat. What I offered her instead was the chance to explore how various foods made her feel, what they represented to her, and how to align her diet with how she wanted to look and feel.

Her quest, her hero's journey, began, as so many do, in the produce department. I met her there during one of our first sessions together to talk about food. We started in the citrus aisle. I asked Stephanie what she thought about oranges. "I think of a cardboard carton in the fridge filled with reconstituted orange juice, extra pulp. My dad loved it. I hated it." She grimaced and I chuckled with a nod. Then I asked her to pick up an orange. She did, and as she held it in her hand, I encouraged her to smell it. Then I took it from her and scraped the rind with my fingernail, which released the fragrant zest and oil. She closed her eyes, bent her head, and took a deep breath. A slow smile spread across her face.

"Nice, huh?" I handed the orange back to her. "Now pass it back and forth between your hands. Tell me what you think is inside of this beautiful ball." She looked around, a little embarrassed that here we were having a deep discussion about a piece of fruit.

"It's really juicy, and sweet, but also kind of tart, where those white threads connect the sections, you know?"

Yes, I nodded.

"They are complicated; sunny and sour," she said.

"Do you like that?" I asked.

"Honestly, I don't know," she replied.

"Want to find out?"

"Why not?" And with that, she put the orange into her basket.

We proceeded through the store at this incredibly leisurely, thoughtful pace for about an hour, and when we got to the checkout, Stephanie found that her basket contained a few things that she did not normally buy: cool, soothing cucumbers; fresh spinach; several varieties of apples; almonds and dates; a bag of limes; some sparkling water . . . and the orange. She promised me that she would really think about how each one tasted, how it made her feel while she ate it, and how she felt afterward. She really wanted to make a connection between what she had selected to eat and how eating it made her feel.

This is intuitive eating. And it is the surest way to optimal health, natural weight loss, and finding pleasure with food.

I had only one request of Stephanie and that was that she stay far away from the scale until we spoke again. She promised me she would do this.

The next week, when we caught up, Stephanie greeted me by saying, "Guess who loves oranges now? And spinach? Who knew?!" The smile on her face told me that they loved her, too.

Several months later and Stephanie's experiment in intuitive eating has been humming along. She's eating a vast array of fruits and vegetables and she's found that she loves tinkering with spices and herbs to create subtle flavor variations in her food. She's become so enamored of this that she told me she had just enrolled in an Indian cooking class for beginners. I was thrilled for her. When we hung up, I felt completely energized and inspired by her.

Almost immediately, my phone rang again — it was Stephanie. "Oh, and I forgot to tell you. I stepped on the scale a few days ago," she said.

"And?" I asked.

"I've lost fifteen pounds. Can you believe it? I mean, Alex, I didn't even try; it just melted away." She sounded so pleased, so at ease. I was thrilled for her.

I reminded her that she did try, but in a completely relaxed and stress-free way; she had learned to engage with food in a way that was all about curiosity and not judgment. Eating had become part of her health care, not an activity she dreaded or something she no longer felt like she had little or no control over. Eating had become, finally, a source of deep pleasure and satisfaction for Stephanie. Her body responded to this loving self-care by letting go of the weight it had felt compelled to stockpile all those years that she had spent dieting.

Download a complimentary Cravings Swap shopping guide at:
www.AlexandraJamieson.com/WFDbonus

CHAPTER SEVEN:
THE IMPORTANCE OF
TRUSTING YOUR GUT

Gut health is the key to overall health.
— Kris Carr

Trust your gut. If you are like me, you've heard this pearl of wisdom whenever you've been on the cusp of making a big life-altering decision. And like me, you may have thought that learning to trust your gut just meant trying to trust your instincts and intuitions. But what if the most influential scientists in the world discovered that trusting your gut meant so much more than that, including that what we know about our brains and how they work has been only partially understood? This is exactly what's happening now, as I write this. The science of neurogastroenterology is quite literally turning everything we think we know about the brain and its role as the master command center of our bodies on its head. All eyes — at least those of neuroscientists —

are now on the gut.

What scientists have long suspected, and are confirming now, is that the stomach and intestines house more neurons than the brain. It is in effect a second brain that is every bit as influential as the one above our shoulders, and understanding this may revolutionize how we approach medicine, nutrition, and healing.

For a few decades, scientists have acknowledged that the health of the brain has a profound effect on the health of our gut, but what they're just now discovering is that the gut also sends out messages of distress (or well-being) to the brain that travel along the vagus nerve, the nervous system's superhighway that runs from the abdomen up to the brain, and that these messages may hold the clue as to how diet and nutrition affect our moods as well as our overall health. This, dear reader, is mind-blowing news.

I think most of us have been very mistaken about how our guts actually work. We tend to think of our gastrointestinal system as being a very primitive sewage system, where something (food) goes in one end, is rudimentarily processed (the extraction of nutrients), and then is eliminated (poop). We've assumed that these are largely fixed, mechanical functions, things that happen automatically without much input from or communication with the brain — or without much input from the gut itself. What science is now showing us is that this is the furthest thing from the truth and that the health and well-being of our gut, which means how we support the digestive process, may very well be the great foundation upon which all wellness rests, including mental wellness.

Well, I certainly believe this, and I've seen firsthand how mindfully caring for your gastrointestinal system will change your life. I've had scores of clients over the past decade tell me that once they cleaned up their gut, they experienced stable moods for the first time in their lives. They left behind fogginess, depression, anxiety, migraines, out-of-control sugar cravings, weight-loss resistance, and persistent sleep issues. These clients were then able to step into a state of mental strength that made things like proactive stress management possible for the first time and they realized that how they treated their gut influenced — quite profoundly — how well their "other" brain was able to perform.

But it's not just our minds that benefit from the proper care and feeding of the gut;

the host of physical ailments that we either ease or fix completely when we take care of our gastrointestinal system is a long one and includes scores of common conditions such as constipation, irritable bowel syndrome, leaky gut, colitis, Crohn's disease, gas, bloating, depression, anxiety, allergies, acne, infertility issues, many autoimmune diseases, obesity, and more. Researchers are discovering that life-threatening ailments such as heart disease, cancer, and type 1 diabetes are all influenced by poor gut health. Learning how to support your gut and not taxing it, we are rapidly learning, is one of the keys, if not *the* key, to vital, strong overall health. And the best way to support your gut is through mindful eating.

THE SECRET GARDEN WITHIN

Your gut is not just wired with complex fine-tuned neural circuitry; it's also teeming with life. You may hear a lot about digestive microbes, flora, bacteria, and yeast — it's enough to make your head spin! What all these words describe are the trillions upon trillions of single-cell organisms that grow and flourish deep within our digestive system, and that are foundational to our immune system health. These organisms, which live in delicate balance with one another, either thrive or die, depending on what we feed them. Scientists call this abundant wild garden of microorganisms the "microbiome," in recognition of the fact that these microbial cells outnumber human cells ten to one in the human body. Think about that for a moment: we are actually made up more of bacterial cells than human cells! The bacterial garden that we host within weighs anywhere from seven ounces to three pounds, depending on our gender, size, and how healthy our gut is. The fact is, our bodies are really just walking shelters that protect this microbial universe and we are just their caretakers. It's up to us to be good hosts and to make sure our gut guests are well cared for. Otherwise they may revolt and trash the place.

The challenges of maintaining gut health are complicated for several reasons. A few generations of eating highly processed diets has led to a depleted pool of healthy bacteria to pass from mother to child. In addition, cesarean deliveries don't allow for natural passage through the birth canal, which is when babies get a major dose of healthy bacteria. Also, women's digestive health is influenced by the major hormonal changes caused by menstruation, childbirth, and menopause, and so it makes sense that as our hormones fluctuate, so does the stability of our gut health. And then there's the underreported fact that stress and anxiety are often felt in the gut, leading to acidity-impaired digestion. Like so much in our lives, our digestive health is not static; it's fluid and changeable and we need to eat and live in ways that acknowledge these changes, however subtle they may be.

WHY YOU NEED TO TEND YOUR INTERNAL GARDEN

Have you ever taken an antibiotic and found that you are suddenly seized with cramping, maybe even some nausea or itching? You may find your appetite is gone or has gone haywire. And that's to be expected, because what antibiotics do is kill all of the microorganisms that are circulating within you — the good and the bad — indiscriminately. Probably your doctor has encouraged you to have some yogurt while you're taking the medication, as the live cultures (aka the substances that support microbe health) in yogurt will begin to repopulate your digestive tract and will jump-start the rebirth of all of those vital, health-promoting cells. Our gut flora is similarly damaged by many other prescription and over-the-counter drugs, like antihistamines, and these further cause the breakdown of our gut health.

While decimating your gut flora with hard-core drugs causes serious health problems, it is just as damaging to let certain types of microbes grow unchecked. I see this problem in women frequently as a condition known as *candida albicans,* which is an overgrowth of intestinal yeasts that thrive on refined sugars and processed foods and is the culprit behind vaginal yeast infections and a long list of other ailments. When any client presents me with evidence of any kind of intestinal bacterial overgrowth, the first food to eliminate is sugar in all of its alluring forms. That's because eating sugar is like throwing a high-powered, toxic fertilizer on the microbes, and those that thrive on sugar will grow out of control, smothering and squeezing out other crucial, health-giving bacteria. The garden becomes overrun with sugar-fed "weeds," and the result is a digestive system that is knocked way out of balance. Once sugar is eliminated from the diet, the resulting return to microbial balance and health is usually swift and certain, and is dramatic enough to convince even the most skeptical clients that maintaining gut health is the game changer and that eliminating sugar is the first step toward balanced digestive health.

I believe candida yeasts and other harmful bacteria actually crave sugar and if they grow unchecked, we become like their zombie slaves, mindlessly fetching anything sugary we can get our hands on to keep them happy. In short, they are the puppet master, and we become their puppets.

What our guts really need are foods that will keep them healthy and able to do their job, which is to break down foods into nutrients and waste. The foods the microbiome really needs and desires are those that provide either the enzymes they need to function or the building blocks needed to create these essential enzymes. These substances are live cultures known as pre- and probiotics.

In the last few years, it's become fashionable for major manufacturers of yogurt products, especially those marketed to women, to add extra, living probiotics to their recipes, and this is a good thing — in theory. That's because the science confirms how good for us probiotics are. What's not so great is that the actual viability of factory-added probiotics is questionable because the mix of probiotics they add to their products is usually limited, and even these few live cultures may be killed or weakened in the heating and preserving processes these mass-produced foods must undergo. But getting probiotics via natural, fresh whole foods, or naturally fermented raw foods, promotes fabulous flora health. So does including prebiotic rich foods (raw foods that contain insoluble fiber, such as onions, leeks, bananas, Jerusalem artichokes, and chicory) that provide food for the helpful bacteria, allowing them to grow and multiply, thereby improving our bodies' ability to absorb key nutrients like calcium and magnesium, and to support the creation and elimination of healthy stools.

Something I'm fascinated by is how ancient cultures, separated by seas and continents, intuitively understood the importance of adding pre- and probiotic foods to their diets. Red wine is a great example of a fermented food that can aid our digestion, as do other fresh, raw fermented foods like sauerkraut and kimchi. Ancient cultures also understood that fermented raw foods (think ancient Greek yogurt) also supported digestive health, and that allowing food to ferment naturally (which means simply allowing the bacteria in the air to interact with the raw vegetables and a little salt) preserved foods, too.

The fermentation process turns sugars

from food into healthful agents like enzymes. The alchemy turns grape juice into wine, grains into beer, carbohydrates into carbon dioxide to leaven sourdough bread, and sugars in vegetables into organic acids, which preserve them.

Ancient Greeks and Romans used sauerkraut (salted shredded cabbage exposed to air) to treat and prevent intestinal infections. Captain Cook and other explorers on the high seas used sauerkraut and lime juice to prevent scurvy. Throughout Europe and Russia sauerkraut and other fermented foods (kefir, yogurt, buttermilk, kvass, borscht, etc.) have been eaten for centuries. Many African cultures still use fermentation as a way of preserving gruels made from corn and sorghum. The people of India use a delicious, pungent paste made from the juice of sauerkraut, as well as yogurt, to aid digestion. Eskimos even bury fermented seal and whale meat to preserve it for use over long, frozen winters.

HANNAH'S STORY

Hannah attended one of my group programs and sought me out afterward to talk one-on-one. She was embarrassed about her problem, because it really affected how she looked. Hannah suffered from a chronic illness, and this meant that she had spent several years taking antibiotics. Though she was now off the drugs, the damage they had done to her digestive system was severe. She suffered from constant, uncomfortable stomach pain, and despite all of her efforts, she hadn't been able to have a regular bowel movement in almost a year. She was also so bloated that she looked about five months pregnant all the time. This was wrecking her self-esteem and putting a huge damper on her social life.

Hannah's gut was sending out a serious SOS. We got together to figure out how to get her on a gut-health diet. We began by doing a quick run-through of what she was currently eating and eliminating all the foods (everything processed, basically) that were adding to her problems with gas, constipation, and cramping. Then we hit the health-food store in search of the solution: supercharged probiotic supplements and raw sauerkraut.

"Uh-oh." Hannah looked leery. "You're not going to suggest I start eating hot dogs, are you?"

I laughed. "No. I want you to use this sauerkraut medicinally; it's loaded with healthy bacteria created by the natural fermentation process, plus, it's got ancient, wilder strains of probiotics in it that you just can't get in even the most sophisticated prepackaged probiotics." I wanted her to start with a tablespoon of kraut per day, preferably with a meal. Then I wanted her to work her way up to having three full tablespoons a day, and if she could, a forkful before her afternoon sugar cravings usually hit.

"Now, two more things: I want you to get a hot-water bottle and fill it up before you go to bed at night. Then I want you to rest it on your tummy. The warmth will draw your body's healing energy toward that part of your anatomy, and I want you to imagine that warmth penetrating your body and melting away all the gunk that's caught up in your gut." She nodded, obediently. "And last . . ." I hesitated. "I want you to go get a vibrator, if you don't have one."

This stopped her cold. "Uh . . . why?" She asked.

"Because having an orgasm will increase the blood flow to the lower part of your body and can help your constipation and cramping."

Hannah looked at me, somewhat stunned. "Well, I actually have one. I just haven't felt like using it because I've felt so gross." I asked her if she'd mind giving it another try.

Two weeks later, Hannah checked in with me. "I don't know if it's the sauerkraut or the vibrator, but I'm pooping regularly for the first time in ages, I'm not feeling nearly as bloated as I did, and I've lost five pounds." I was impressed. "Plus, I'm feeling kind of spunky and alive again." If we weren't on the phone, I would have winked at her.

THE RHYTHM OF DIGESTION

There is something beautifully rhythmic about our daily digestive cycle that I encourage all of my clients to learn about and embrace. If our digestive system is functioning well, we'll have at least one healthy bowel movement every day and we won't suffer from uncomfortable conditions like gas, bloating, cramping, constipation, or diarrhea. On top of eliminating these distressing symptoms, when our digestive tract is healthy, our bodies are able to better absorb nutrients, process and eliminate toxins, effortlessly maintain healthy body weight, and perform well physically and mentally. To build the respect our digestive systems deserve from us, I find it's helpful to get a working understanding of what our digestive system actually looks like and how, in very simple terms, it works.

The gut is the flexible cellular tube that runs from the mouth to the anus, and when fully extended, the average human adult gut measures about twenty-six feet in length. Flattened out, this thin, stretchy tissue would cover an area roughly the size of a football field. This is some serious real estate, and we rarely take the time to think about the processes of digestion that occur all along the way within this massive container of microbial life.

Few of us know that digestion is happening all the time, even when we sleep. But it does follow a waking day cycle that begins when our feet first hit the ground in the morning. That's why starting the day with at least one tall glass of warm water and lemon is so important and is recommended in countless formal diet plans. This refreshing drink rehydrates us after a long night of respirating water through our breath and pores. It also preps the liver and gall bladder for the hard work of the day ahead, which entails keeping our bodies free of impurities and toxins. The lemon primes our enzymes to fire up and stirs our other digestive organs to waken and prepare for the day's work. Then it's on to breakfast, the meal that sets the tone and tempo for how your digestion, and your energy, will proceed for the rest of the day.

The moment food hits our tongue, our gut goes to work when key digestive enzymes that reside in saliva are activated and begin to break down food. That's why being aware of the action of chewing is such an important aspect of mindful eating; if we gulp our food, rather than macerate it enough so it can be fully steeped in the mouth's enzymes, we skip right over a vital step in the process of digestion. Learning this tidbit is an eye-opener for most of my clients, who thought that being told to "slow down and chew your food" was a technique most diets employed in order to get them to eat less. Though eating less may be a nice by-product of chewing more deliberately, the real benefit is that it gives the body the chance to start extracting beneficial nutrients from food right off the bat, and it begins the process of breaking down food cells into waste, so elimination will be regular and healthy.

When we chew mindfully, we prepare the food for its next stop in the stomach, where digestion really gets ramped up. The stomach is a unique organ that is lined with cell membranes that keep powerful acids and enzymes contained and undiluted so digestion can work optimally. When we eat digestion-disrupting foods (which, research shows, means any foods that are highly processed, refined, and devoid of the pre- or probiotics found in fresh, whole foods) that are antagonistic to the microbes we need to keep the stomach lining and the gut lining intact, we put ourselves at risk of breaking down the linings of the stomach. If this happens, our guts may begin leaking all sorts of chemicals and toxins into our circulatory system, causing disease-inducing inflammation, brain fog, and even mood disruption. When our bodies are internally irritated in this way, when they become inflamed, we become susceptible to a whole host of awful ailments, from metabolic syndrome (obesity, high blood pressure, pre-diabetes), to autoimmune conditions such as rheumatoid arthritis and thyroid disease, and even to cancer.

This is why keeping your gut acids and enzymes contained is crucial. So, too, is making sure you don't dilute these acids once you've finished eating and your stomach goes into full digestion mode. If you drink too much water with a meal, your digestive juices can be diluted and stall the process and you'll just feel miserable, waterlogged, and bloated all at once. I know this sounds counter to what most diets tell you, which is to drink a minimum of eight glasses of water a day, and of course this is a good thing — but not when your belly is full. In fact, health philosophies, such as Chinese medicine, believe that if you drink too much cold liquid, you'll actually extinguish the digestive fire. So even being mindful of when you take in your hydration is crucial to digestive health, too.

Just as not chewing your food well enough can limit nutrient delivery and hinder digestion, overeating also throws a wrench in the works. When you overindulge, you overwhelm your stomach on many fronts — by taxing its physical capacity, by diluting the available enzymes, and so on. Overeating is like asking a woman who has never lifted to hoist a five-hundred-pound barbell over her head; it's such a shock to the system that it causes your metabolism to fail and your system is left with no choice but to rapidly convert all of that excess nutritional byproduct into fat — all that excess food mass has to go somewhere, right? And if your digestive system is calibrated to work at a certain pace, and to accommodate only a certain volume, well, it can only handle so much overdrive before it just starts to sputter and quit.

So eating manageable portions — rather than supersizing — or even small portions over a twelve-hour day (think 7 a.m. to 7 p.m.) is most desirable. Then, when evening comes and you feel comfortably satisfied, you can head off to sleep knowing that you're resting your body and soul and your gut, too.

GENTLY BREAKING THE FAST

One of the things my clients love so much about undergoing a detox is that it provides them with a clean slate. Once they've taken foods that cause irritation out of their diets, they love how calm and relaxed their systems are and how calm and relaxed they feel around food.

When we're eating mindlessly in response to our habits and cravings, there is an amped-up urgency clouding our relationship to food, an anxiety that corrupts our ability to make good choices. Food should never cause panic. In fact, when we approach food from a place of calm, which is what a detox prepares us to do, we expect that it is going to make us feel good.

Eating to feel good, for many women, upends their lifelong love-hate relationship with food in ways that can genuinely and profoundly change their lives. When they've cleared their digestive system, they've also, as a happy by-product, dismantled a lot of the mental wiring that had eating and food all tangled up with stress, feelings of inadequacy, fears involving scarcity — so many negative hooks around food are deactivated by detoxing. In short, we get to begin anew with food, and the best place to do this is with the first meal of the day.

It's generally accepted that eating breakfast is a wise and healthy thing to do, but the reasons for this are unclear to most women who struggle with their weight or with feeling comfortable in their bodies. That's because we've been conditioned to think of food only in terms of calories, a benign measure of energy that has confused most of us about the fact that we need food to support us, even in our efforts to lose weight. When our thinking about food becomes hijacked by the belief that food equals fat, we forget that food is our best ally in healing ourselves and improving our health, which may include losing excess body fat. I think this is especially true where breakfast is concerned.

I know the way I nutritionally prepare my body for the day ahead excites me. While I'm having my lemon water (which always seems to clear away any sleepiness and helps me feel instantly energized), I think about what's on the schedule for the next few hours and how I want to feel during these hours. Since I've been writing this book, I know that I want to be focused, clearheaded, and nimble — the idea of ingesting anything too heavy or food-coma-inducing just doesn't feel appealing. So I've been starting my days with green and lean protein smoothies that combine energy-grounding protein with whatever favorite raw, whole foods I have at hand. This might mean a handful of kale, blended with an apple, some good-quality protein, and maybe a bit of coconut oil or half an avocado. I include whatever strikes my fancy. Then I take small sips. I let my taste buds linger and identify every flavor they find, and then I chew. Yes — you heard right; I'm one of those people who chews her smoothies. This actually came up recently when a client, Lucy, wrote to say that she didn't know what to do with herself when her morning smoothie was gone in about ninety seconds. I picked up the phone and called her so we could talk about this.

First, I asked her how downing her breakfast in a few big, fast gulps made her feel. Her answer: full yet dissatisfied. Then I asked her why she felt like she had to race through her breakfast. I knew she had to get her kids off to school and then get to her office, but for Lucy, it wasn't about not having enough time to slow down her breakfast ritual — something else was going on.

"I guess . . ." Her voice was faltering, "I haven't felt like I deserved to relax. My husband makes fun of the 'gross green goop' I've got to choke down and so I feel kind of ashamed, you know, like I don't get to eat 'normal' food."

Actually, I didn't know, because my own partner *loves* my deep-green morning shakes, precisely because they help us both feel good. He gets a blast of nutrition without feeling full and gross and he finds it's a great way to start his workday. "Has he ever tried your green goop?" I asked.

She laughed. "He should — it tastes good and has just the right amount of sweet, and they help me feel great all morning." I suggested to her that even though her first meal of the day was in a glass, she should approach having it as she would every meal; that she sit down, with her kids and husband, and enjoy it while they were all having a bigger, more traditional breakfast. I also suggested that the rest of her family at least try her drink — mostly so they'd understand that she wasn't having a glass of liquid torture. I told her to call me the next day.

Lucy checked in with me the following day in the late morning. She sounded fabulous. "I'm between meetings at work and I only have a minute, but I wanted to tell you that I enjoyed my smoothie for about a half hour today. Eating it in a slow, relaxed way" — yes, she used the word "eat" — "felt so luxurious and good — I even used a pretty wineglass to serve it in! My husband and kids saw the new glass and actually asked for a sip! I left the house feeling calmer and satisfied and not rushed and bloated."

I was thrilled to hear this. Lucy had tuned into how she was approaching her food, how she was eating it, in a way that reset her habit of eating fast and furiously and getting too full too fast. This is an incredibly important skill for all of us to have, and understanding what "full" means is crucial to getting out from under cravings, learning to enjoy food, and most important, supporting healthy digestion.

It took me half my life to finally get a handle on what being full means. I had always equated being full with being stuffed to the gills, with also being utterly hopped up on sugar or caffeine (or both). It meant being uncomfortably numb, bloated, and heavy. And tired. It wasn't until my own first detox at twenty-five that I realized that the sensations I used to describe "full" were extreme ones and that there is a subtler, healthier, more gentle and loving way to know when you've had enough food.

I find it helpful to share a hungry-full scale with my clients, with zero being empty, five being neutral, and ten being bursting. If we wait until we are at zero to eat, we're so ravenous that we have no sense of control or moderation or discretion. This is a state I call being "hangry," because if we get this depleted, we are often on the verge of an angry meltdown (both physically and mentally). When we fall toward zero on the hungry-full spectrum, then we'll eat *anything* we can get our hands on, and this is when we speed to the drive-through or grab the cookies hiding in the back of the freezer.

So we want to avoid zero at all costs. I find it takes most of my clients a bit of time and experimentation to really get a handle on what five, or being "hunger neutral," feels like. When most people detox, they find that their own sense of scale had until then been pretty out of whack. Getting to a clean slate and being able to familiarize yourself with what it truly feels like to be satiated, or digestively content, is a gift we rarely give ourselves.

Being free from reacting to food and no longer being prisoner to our habits and cravings allows us to tune into ourselves and our appetites in really intimate, empowering ways, and once you land on this neutral midpoint between truly starving and over-stuffed, you find that you can relax around food in profound ways — maybe for the first time in your life. From this easy, grounded place, you can make much more mindful choices about how, when, and what you will eat.

The midpoint on the hungry-full scale is the sweet spot on the nutritional continuum, the balance point, the place where we're likely to experience our bodies and the world with satisfaction and acceptance. This is the point where hunger vanishes and we lose our obsessive awareness of food. From here, you become free to notice subtleties and variations in how you feel that you weren't available to experience when you were eating in a more volatile all-or-nothing way. For example, you may find that when you wake up, you feel that you are at a relatively comfortable four, so you decide to enjoy just water or tea for the first hour or so of the day, allowing your body to rehydrate before you eat any food. You may wait to eat until you reach a more compelling three, when you decide it is time for breakfast. I have one client, Jane, who doesn't really hit this place until late, late morning, and that's okay; she has breakfast when a lot of us are already thinking about lunch.

The goal with breakfast — or any meal for that matter — is to bring us just up past five to a really pleasant six or seven, and when we hit eight, we pretty much know it's time to stop. Getting into nine or ten territory means certain misery that may manifest in several undesirable ways including cramping, bloating, gas, nausea, fatigue, brain fuzziness, and weight gain.

Finding balance on the hungry-full scale is all about moderation and staying on the middle path. It's about checking in with ourselves gently and regularly about what we need. When we do this, we find that eating actually soothes and energizes, rather than stresses. When we stay in that comfortable midrange, we feel enlivened, not weighted down, by food. This is when we feel healthy and supported — not harmed — by what we eat. Striving for this smooth, fluid, easy relationship with food is the goal, because our relationship with food ought to be a happy and harmonious one, always.

THE LUNCH CONUNDRUM

Let's do lunch. I mean really — let's talk about lunch in ways that we never, ever do. I know very few adults, except for myself and a lucky few friends, who work for themselves and so have access to their own kitchens during the day. Everyone else is out there in the work world, on the clock, with limited time and limited options when it comes to the important work of feeding themselves. This meal we call lunch, it seems to me, is the toughest to do right, given that it's shoehorned into the middle of our crazy busy day.

Oh, to live in a rural Mediterranean village, where lunch is a time for putting work aside, gathering around an abundant table, and connecting with family and loved ones over a leisurely, thoughtfully prepared meal. For many cultures, lunch is the big food experience of the day, and it is often followed by a period of rest (siesta, anyone?). This is an acknowledgment of how taxing digestion is and how by quieting down our lives after a big meal we give our bodies a chance to metabolize the bounty it just received. It's too bad that this isn't the way we approach lunch here.

Grabbing lunch nowadays is the antithesis of the Mediterranean midday meal. Most of us are so busy that we're lucky if we can get our hands on something as "healthy" as a PowerBar and a bottle of water at lunchtime. And that's only when we are lucky. But if we don't figure out a way to power-up with a protein-rich, veggie-heavy, healthful meal midday, we are at risk for the blood sugar/energy crash that usually hits all of us sometime between 2 and 5 p.m. Then when we're at this horrible low late in the afternoon, we tend to scramble for quick energy in the form of coffee or candy or nutrient-poor snack foods like chips, cookies, and so on. This is a really dangerous time for our digestive system, when what our bodies really need is something fresh and nutritious. As for Jane, my late-morning breakfast client? Since Jane has a healthy, rather big breakfast late, she works at her desk through the lunch rush, then takes a hand-packed meal out to the park across the street from her office and sits in the sun from 3 to 4 p.m., enjoying something she prepared at home, usually a delicious leftover from the previous night's dinner, repurposed as a salad or wrap. When Jane gets home, around 6:30, she usually has a light supper, followed by a fresh piece of fruit, and drifts off to sleep around 9 p.m., feeling what she calls "a perfect five."

WHAT'S FOR DINNER?

I would say that the biggest change for me since I healed my own relationship to food is how I approach dinner. I grew up in a traditional American family where dinner was the biggest meal of the day. But that's changed for me, as I've become the head of my own household and my self-care regarding food has improved so much. I am a big believer that gathering with loved ones at the end of the day is one of the great joys of life. What I no longer believe is that eating a heavy, dense meal at this gathering is always the way to go. Even as the mother of a young child, I've learned to reject the pressure to fill a plate and you definitely won't find me pushing anyone to finish their food, especially if it's meant to signify that they liked it. The "clean plate club" is one I just don't want to be a member of.

We eat early in my household, usually sometime around 6 p.m., and not just because there are young ones around. We eat at this time because we all feel best if we don't go to bed on a full stomach, and I especially enjoy having a hot cup of tea and some quiet time before I hit the hay. For dinner, I like to provide an array of fresh, locally grown organic foods that provide a nutritionally rich and delicious experience. On some days, this may mean having a full meal; on others, for me it might be another green and clean smoothie, a salad, some nuts, and a healthy fat, like avocado or some smoked salmon, if I'm only about a four on the hunger scale at that time. No one in my family wants to know if something is wrong when my appetite tells me that I need more of a snack than a full meal; on the contrary, eating in response to what my body tells me it needs indicates to my loved ones that my self-caring skills are working just fine. There's no judgment there, no force-feeding or scolding or cajoling. Even my elementary schooler knows when enough is enough — except, of course, when chocolate chip cookies are involved.

The goal of eating — always — is to best support our daily digestion in a way that mindfully keeps our hunger-fullness scale from tipping too drastically from one extreme to another. It should also be a really pleasant experience, in terms of taste. Gathering with good people and breaking bread is one of life's great pleasures, and we ought to approach each meal with gratitude, acknowledging how very lucky we are to have so much good, healthy food available to us. Slow and steady, in eating as with so many things in life, is absolutely the desirable way to go.

Dinnertime is a time of really delicious detoxing in my home. We leave our phones and devices far from the table when we gather, and I usually (even at breakfast) light a candle or two to signify the gratitude I feel for the people around me and the food we're sharing. We take the time to talk about our day and to talk about food, too. It's our time to connect and get the emotional nourishment we need as well.

Get Alex's favorite Clean, Lean & Green Protein smoothie recipes at:
www.AlexandraJamieson.com/WFD
bonussmoothies

CHAPTER EIGHT:
RELISHING YOUR BODY'S CAPACITY FOR PLEASURE

Oh, how I regret not having worn a bikini for the entire year I was twenty-six. If anyone young is reading this, go, right this minute, put on a bikini, and don't take it off until you're thirty-four.

— Nora Ephron

Women should own their sexuality.

— Beyoncé

I love the writer and filmmaker Nora Ephron, and I miss her. She really got it that we are way too hard on ourselves and she had the hindsight when she was older to cop to the fact that we miss out on feeling foxy when we most have the God-given right to because we're so damn hard on ourselves. And I'm grateful that there are incredible women like Beyoncé stepping into their feminine power and their sexuality with such grace. She, like Nora, understands that

230

all of us deserve to feel foxy and good in our bodies at any weight, any age, any time of the month. Period. Much of my work is helping my clients to see that they deserve to feel this way, too, no matter how much they weigh, what their relationship status is, or for any other reason. Beauty is our birthright, but it is so, so difficult for us to really accept this.

In some ways helping my clients learn body acceptance is the hardest part of my job. I believe we're so hard on ourselves in large part because the culturally sanctioned images of what is beautiful seem to be contracting, rather than expanding, and now, in the age of the selfie, no one can escape the pressures of the camera and the tyranny of air-brushing, nipping, tucking, waxing, plucking, bleaching — all the painful and expensive things we do to ourselves in order to look a certain way, which is the rigid way the media tells us we should look. None of us can move an inch without coming up short because the so-called standards of what "looks good" have become so artificial and unattainable.

That's why I tell my clients, even as they're beginning to detox their bodies of the foods that compromise how well they feel, that they need to detox from the media, too, and take a breather from all the images of emaciated models and glam-squad-attended celebrities, whom none of us in a million years will ever look like. I encourage them to avoid going online, watching TV, and looking at magazines, just for a while, to get to know themselves and to feel the pleasure they're capable of, to tap into their own inner beauty, once and for all. Because if we don't figure out how to love ourselves now, we're all just going to end up feeling like shit about ourselves until it's all over, no matter how well, fit, rested, and sexy we really are.

The researcher and writer Brené Brown talks about how, of all the pressures we face, concerns about our appearance and weight are the number-one shame triggers for women. "Feeling bad about our neck," to paraphrase Ephron's book title, or our butts or our thighs or our wrinkles, has become a terrible, entrenched habit for most of us. And this brutal habit siphons off the best of what we've got to offer by overshadowing and minimizing all the good things we've got to give to the world. Body shame keeps an invisible glass wall between us and life. It hampers our ability to thrive in all arenas: in the boardroom, the bedroom, the back-yard. Body shame robs us of so much of the good stuff in life; it cripples our ability to truly take in a compliment; it makes it impossible to enjoy a sensual experience without self-censorship; it inhibits our ability to let loose and play and run and jump and dance and sing with true abandon. Shame sucks. And body shame is the worst.

I encourage my clients to understand that fighting for radical body acceptance is a bold, political move and that it exemplifies the wisdom of putting the oxygen mask on yourself first. Hating oneself for not having a "perfect" body means we're automatically hating our neighbor, too, for the very same, lame reasons. We have to make peace with ourselves, right here, right now, or we're never going to be okay with ourselves, with food, with sex, with anything truly worthwhile in life. And we're not going to allow our girlfriends, mothers, sisters, or daughters to be okay, either. The body hating has to stop. And first, it has to stop with you.

BODY ALIENATION STARTS YOUNG

"I just want to at least *like* the way I look." Jessica Ann said this with utter resignation in her voice, while I had to consciously keep my jaw from dropping, because Jessica Ann is one of the most radiant, sexy, healthy, and vital women I know. I'd known her now for many months, but it was still hard for me to understand how unforgiving Jessica Ann was about her own appearance. Given her upbringing, though, it wasn't hard to figure out where she'd learned this.

Jessica Ann had been raised in a strict, conservative household, the oldest of four children and the only girl. Her mother, who worked at home, was anxious that Jessica Ann be a "lady" and not the crazy, fearless tomboy (who could outrun, outthrow, and outwit her brothers at most games) that she was. So her mother went overboard the other way, forcing dresses and ribbons and glamour on Jessica Ann. Then, when puberty hit and all of Jessica Ann's natural womanliness started to emerge, her mother panicked and began relentlessly shaming her daughter about being too alluring and too provocative, when in fact Jessica Ann was simply being herself. To silence her mother, Jessica Ann took to wearing hoodies and old jeans, and to seek out emotional comfort in food. When I met her, she'd lost forty of the fifty pounds she'd been hauling around for most of her life and she wanted my support while she lost the last ten. She had contacted me because she knew that when she gave up the last of her "armor" — which is what she called those last ten pounds — she'd have to allow herself to be physically vulnerable in the world in ways that now, in her thirties, terrified her.

"I just don't know if I can take any more of that intense criticism," she said during our phone session. "About my boobs being too big or my clothes not being conservative enough. I just couldn't win with my mom. I remember getting ready for the fall dance in junior high, and when I came downstairs, she actually said, in front of my date, 'You're going out in that?' I was wearing a dress that I'd borrowed from my older cousin; it was a simple, pretty long gown she'd worn to a friend's wedding. I remember not understanding what the problem was — the dress fit me perfectly, I felt appropriate and pretty, my date seemed to think I looked nice . . ." At this point her voice trailed off.

"Whenever my mother made comments like this, I just felt wrong. Like the body I was born into was wrong. Do you know what I mean?" She had gotten the message, however unintentionally, that becoming a woman just wasn't okay. So she started to hide her curves, to bury her femininity under baggy clothes, and she unconsciously began to build a barricade between her body and the rest of the world by overeating and putting on a layer of fat. This became her way of avoiding criticism — and contact with others.

Jessica Ann's story really tears at my heart because so many of us learned body shame from our very own mothers. I spent a lot of time working with her trying to explain what her mother might have meant, but in the end, we just couldn't find anything of value there. What we did come away with was this: whenever we criticize how someone looks (ourselves or another), we are failing to see that person at all. When we say snarky things about the way a woman carries herself (including if she may be carrying more weight than we think she should), we are rejecting her, straight up. Shame is all about rejection, and when we're constantly shaming ourselves, we're making ourselves unavailable for all of the good stuff life has to offer, including real, juicy intimacy. I believe Jessica Ann's mother was trying to protect her from the sometimes-violent realities of sex, which scare most women, and Jessica Ann turned that subconscious fear into a protective, physical barrier of fat.

Jessica Ann, like so many of us, had been buried under the heavy weight of body shame for most of her life and it had affected everything: her relationship to food, her feelings about her desirability as a woman, her intimate relationships with men. In short, her lack of love for her own body had kept her from feeling joy and living a passionate, playful life. Learning to step out of the shadow of that shame was, she knew, the most important work she would ever do; not relying on food to provide armor against a man and the trials of life would make her vulnerable, but it would also set her free. Finally, Jessica Ann was beginning to understand this.

We're all up against it, in our culture, in terms of feeling validated for how we look. Who among us can compete with Barbie or Bratz? Even when our mothers love their own bodies and so model for us how to love ours, still we're relentlessly pressured to be thinner, blonder, bluer-eyed (truthfully; the ideal for beauty in this country has been studied, and it's a very monocultural, very pale ideal indeed). Girls have a shorter and shorter window of opportunity to just be wild-animal children, while women who are over forty are pressured to erase all signs of aging before they even have the chance to let life find their faces. Every now and then, when I'm waiting at the checkout line in the grocery store, I'll see a picture of an older woman, someone who had once been a star of the screen, and her face will be so taut and unrecognizable that it fills me with a sense of shame and dread.

It's just not easy living in a woman's body in this world, and I'm not so sure we can blame men for this. Besides, finding someone to blame simply misses the point; it doesn't matter where all of these messed-up messages come from — we've got to reject them, one and all.

MAKING IT OKAY TO BE A HEALTHY WOMAN

I think part of the reason Jessica Ann's mother panicked when she began to transform from a girl into a woman is that we are very threatened by a woman who owns her own power, be it political, economic, or sexual. Sheryl Sandberg writes about this in her bestseller, *Lean In,* a conversation she started about why there aren't more women in leadership roles in business. She talks about how when a man makes a firm decision, he's considered a "leader," and when he asks for a raise, he's commended; yet when a woman makes the same kind of gestures, she's considered a "bitch." No wonder we don't make a play for the corner office; none of us want to be characterized as being a bitch or cold or bossy or any other negative thing just because we do or say something with conviction. For God's sake, the truth is, we are none of these things. And we're sick and tired of being pelted with labels — so tired, in fact, that many of us have just given up and let ourselves be buried beneath them. Finding our way to caring for ourselves around food is related to this kind of submission. I see it often in women who actually don't want to lose the last of their armor weight because they've become utterly convinced that without it, they'll be too powerful, too threatening, too much to those around them.

If a woman were to give up the weight that's masking her power, she would become more nimble, more noticeable, more visible in ways that would force her to be more accountable for, and in, her life.

And being accountable scares us. And no wonder, because if we become accountable, we run the risk of becoming seen and successful, and if we become successful . . . no one will like or love us. Or that's how some version of that thinking goes, but it's time for us to reject this kind of chatter as the toxic nonsense that it is.

Owning our power is where it's at, regardless of what our mothers, our sisters, our colleagues — all the other women in our life — believe. It's up to us to take the bold first step into our power, so we can model for one another how it's done. And I, like Sheryl Sandberg, believe it will go viral, this learning to love powerful women, if we only give it a chance. Learning to love your body is the crucial first step in claiming your personal power. I believe that none of us have to be girlish (diminutive, quiet, and sweet) as opposed to womanly (voluptuous, verbal, and brave) in order to be loved and accepted.

BRINGING SEXY BACK

One of the aspects of body shame that nearly crippled me and that has caused countless women so much unhappiness is how it has affected their ability to have and enjoy sex. This is absolutely parallel to and tied up with our ability — or inability — to enjoy and find pleasure in food. In both instances, feeling ashamed of these relation-ships manifests in our not being honest about who we are and what we need.

Most women who overeat do so to find some kind of emotional solace that they aren't getting from themselves or from other people. Or they do so in order to, however unconsciously, render themselves unattractive in ways that give them a way of opting out of taking responsibility for their sexual selves. Conversely, women who starve themselves are doing the same thing, but by going in the other direction, they are willing to literally make themselves disappear in order to achieve unhealthy standards of sexy.

What all of us need to really embrace is that sex isn't about what your body looks like — it's about how it feels. And sex is about a body feeling good.

I feel pretty darn lucky. I grew up in a household where sex wasn't flaunted, but it wasn't hidden, either. I understood, pretty early on, that sex was a natural, healthy part of life and that it was happening right there in the home I lived in. But that's not to say that I was well prepared for my own budding sexuality, either. I was lucky that I lived in a good school district that offered a yearlong sex-education class for all the fifth graders, boys and girls. My teacher, Mrs. Brown, just happened to be pregnant for most of the year, and this made it easy for her to talk about sex in a really matter-of-fact and nonthreatening way. At the start of the year, she put a cardboard box on the corner of her desk and told us that at any point during the year we could write down a question about sex or our bodies and drop it into the box, anonymously. Then she would read the question to the whole class and answer it, since if one of us wanted to know something specific, she was sure that others of us wanted that same information, too.

I don't know what prompted me to do it, but one day I wrote down a question and when everyone was filing out of the room, I furtively dropped it into the box. The next day, when it was time for sex ed, Mrs. Brown reached into the box and pulled out a question: "What would happen if you swallowed semen?" It was my question!

I turned bright red as the rest of the class erupted with laughter. I have no idea why I asked this, but I do remember feeling relieved to learn that a woman could not get pregnant from swallowing sperm. That's how little, at eleven, I knew about sex.

A couple of years later, when puberty finally hit, it seemed as though I had walked through an invisible curtain and into a much more serious, much darker world. I remember a girl in our grade, who was no more than twelve at the time, telling us on the playground that her uncle made her have sex with him. I was so frightened by this that I jumped off the swing and ran away! (Fortunately, another classmate told one of our teachers about this.) Around this time, I got my period for the first time, and of course it started while I was at school. We had swimming for gym that day, and all year our gym teacher had been drilling it into us girls that we could do everything — including swimming — when we had our period. But I didn't have any tampons and even if I did, I didn't really know how to use them. The school nurse gave me a giant pad to put in my pants, so I had to sit in the bleachers while everyone else swam. It was humiliating and confusing.

Pretty soon I started to think about boys and to masturbate, and before long, I was making out with some of the boys, but only those who I knew would keep our little rendezvous secret. Even in the 1980s, in Portland, I didn't want to get a reputation as being "slutty," but I wanted to know what boys smelled like, what they felt like, what they tasted like. I just didn't want to be judged by anyone else — especially my girlfriends — for being curious about sex, even way back then.

A friend of mine recently went to hear Gloria Steinem speak, and at the end of the talk, a young woman, a high school senior, told Ms. Steinem that there was a lot of pressure among her peers to perform oral sex on the boys they liked. Ms. Steinem asked the young woman, "Well, that may be so, but what's in it for you?" My friend said the audience erupted in applause, as Ms. Steinem was asking the essential yet too often unspoken question: "Yes, my dear, but what about *your* pleasure?"

Female sexual pleasure is still a terrifying and taboo topic. And it's definitely one that's far too complicated to cover fully here, but it's one we need to begin to really openly and honestly talk about, because I truly believe that the full expression of female desire and pleasure — including our need for hot sex — is at the heart of our health and well-being.

And I'm talking about pleasure in all of its full-bodied glory, which includes the pleasure we should experience from our relationship with food. This is where food and sex become so linked, so intertwined. When sex becomes too dangerous for us to fully enjoy, food becomes our version of safe sex. Many of the very healthy needs and desires we have for touch, intimacy, and sex get funneled into the furtive, addictive, and unhealthy habits we build around food. Food has become one of the only acceptable means of quenching our desires, but at tremendous cost to our relationships with our own bodies.

The intense pressure we're under to be perceived as desirable, in an objectified way, has us either starving ourselves to meet an unrealistic ideal, or gorging ourselves so we don't have to feel how lonely or sexually unfulfilled we may be. On both ends of this spectrum, there is a world of hurt and unrelenting shame that I want women to break free of.

I know. I have been there. And it's an awful, dark, lonely place to be.

When I was a young teen, I discovered, much to my delight, boys and their bodies. I wanted to explore things with them, and yet this healthy, natural desire sent me underground, like it does so many young women. Now, I didn't come of age in a family or time or culture that insisted I had to be a virgin until I married my one true love, but nonetheless . . . I didn't grow up in a culture that taught me how to celebrate my blossoming sexuality, either. I wasn't encouraged to own my sexuality in empowering and healthy ways. So once I kissed a boy and I liked it, and then I kissed another, and another, I hid all of this from everyone — my parents, my friends — everyone. I held off on having sex until I was almost eighteen and was in love with my then-long-term boyfriend, and I feel grateful that my first experience of sexual intercourse was such a safe and happy one. Despite my trauma-free early sexual experience, like most women, I have had periods of really losing touch with my sexuality, of losing my sense of myself as a worthy and desirable being, and when this has happened, I've lost touch with the most vital and authentic parts of myself.

I really felt this kind of sexual shame when I learned that my husband was cheating on me. Even before then, I found myself feeling lonely and abandoned in my marriage as his work had him on the road pretty much all of the time. So I was home alone with our newborn, sexually frustrated and missing him in ways that were really difficult, and at times, nearly unbearable. I missed my randy partner, the guy who had swept me off my feet and with whom I'd discovered so much about life and love. When he finally came home and we had a stretch of time together, I began to doubt my attractiveness, as he no longer initiated sex with me. I started to feel inadequate, but I didn't know why. When I pressed him on it, he made excuses about being tired or overworked or stressed out. In short, he shut me out. I didn't know what to do or how to reconnect with him, and so my doubts about my own desirability festered and grew. Then I found out; he'd been sleeping with someone he'd met through work, and when I asked him about this person, he told me he thought he might be in love with her.

At that moment, my world fell apart. But what I lost wasn't just my husband; I lost myself. I lost myself in a terrible black hole of shame. It was the shame of rejection, the shame of no longer being desired. It was devastating. And I went numb.

My life shifted then in ways that were really dislocating. I moved into a smaller apartment with my baby and began to grope around, trying to piece together and rebuild my life. I found myself just feeling much less safe in the world and definitely not at all at home in my own skin. Now, when I'd be walking along and a random catcall would come my way, it felt like a slap, instead of something I could just brush off. I found that being objectified in any way, even when it was meant to be a compliment, exacerbated how lousy I felt about myself. It wasn't until much later, when I was on the other side of this, that I realized that betrayal has this way of distorting and dismantling things in ways that were frightening and unfamiliar to me; the sense of losing control, or more accurately, having no control over the trajectory of my life, terrified me. I thought seriously about leaving my adopted city of New York and heading back home to Portland, Oregon; I wanted to just cut and run and give up on my life there, believing that if I went home, I'd somehow feel safer.

But I knew this was no real solution and that running out on my life, as wrecked as it was, would be running out on myself. And so I stayed. And I learned to stay with myself even when I felt like a wobbly, fragile mess.

The next several years were a time of deep discovery; about who I am, what I believe, what I really want from life. I knew that I wanted to experience deep love and intimacy with a man again, but I felt locked out of love — literally. My libido was frozen, as though my husband's rejection had been a stun gun that had been aimed directly at my G spot. I had no idea how to access the part of me that felt playful and sexy. I didn't know how to feel at home in my body again. I felt injured and alone, and finding my way out of this deep isolation took a few years and a lot of hard work.

First, I had to really acknowledge that I had sexual desires and that these were healthy and important. I was able to connect with guides and coaches and friends who encouraged me to talk openly about these things, to break through the taboos that had kept me so secretive and isolated about this topic.

I found that at first, talking openly about lust, attraction, desire — all of it — made me really nervous and, of course, embarrassed and self-conscious. But before too long, it made me feel energized and empowered — and alive. I realized that I was being coached to approach my sexual desires with openness and curiosity — which is the same way I encourage my clients to approach food. I was advised, by the remarkable team of Ariel and Shya Kane, whose workshop, Monday Night Alive!, provided me with the community and support I needed to break my isolation, that it was important that I approach men and dating with no judgment and no expectations. I needed to stay firmly planted in a frame of mind that was about listening — especially listening to my body and how it felt in the company of whomever I was meeting. Again, this is exactly how I advise my clients to approach food. The Kanes stressed that meeting someone once — just once, for just an hour — would give me a lot of important information about myself, including information that might lead to real, meaningful internal change and much healthier relationships with others. I thought about all the times I'd encourage my clients to just give kale a chance, and I knew I had to do it, even though I hadn't been on a date in many, many years.

And so I began to date and explore and get to know my sexual self in a new, non-judgmental way. It was the most liberating period of my life. Being a good mother was my highest priority, so I was able to bypass putting any pressure on myself to find "the one" or to seek out any kind of committed relationship. Instead, I followed my instincts and engaged with men in a consensual, playful, stress-free way. It was an incredibly healthy time in my life, and it was during this phase of dating that I was able to reintegrate into my body, to regain my sense of myself as an attractive and desirable woman, one who was just beginning to learn about her own deep needs and desires.

I recently did the math, and during that two-year period after my divorce, I went on about a hundred first dates. Most of those, of course, were also last dates, but that was how it was supposed to be. It was so helpful to meet a man in a coffee shop and know, after a few minutes of chatting, that we weren't meant to get to know each other beyond that meeting. I did connect with a few men and I had sexual relationships with some, but I never committed to just one man. At least not until I met Bob, my current partner.

When I first met Bob, I was struck by how open and frank he was. He told me, right off the bat, that before he moved to New York, he had been living in a community that was all about healthy, open sex. My brain heard "sex cult!" but instead of running, I listened. He told me that he liked to play in the BDSM world (erotic practices that include bondage, dominance, role-playing — a whole host of yummy, fun, and titillating things). He looked me straight in the eye as he told me this, and let me tell you . . . it was hot! I wanted to end our date and rush home with him immediately. He did invite me over, showed me a couple of neat rope tricks — and I nearly lost my mind with desire. But he wouldn't sleep with me. Not yet. He wanted us to get to know one another, to really talk about what we wanted from a sexual partner, with sex, with our own bodies.

Where had this man come from?

I had never, in all my life, had such a deep, meaningful, and frank conversation with someone about sex. With Bob, I dipped my toe into the world of BDSM, made famous by the wildly best-selling *Fifty Shades of Grey* books. At first, I was nervous. Stepping into parties where the guests were tying each other up in rope corsets, or acting out predetermined scenes, à la Stanley Kubrick's *Eyes Wide Shut,* frightened and excited me. Once I started talking to people, though, I realized that I could feel safe. These were actually sweet, honest people interested in creating fantasies around sex that would allow consenting adults to take their pleasure to the edge, without the risk of falling off the cliff. The people I have encountered in this world tend to be mature and clear about their sexual desires, and I find this to be incredibly hot and fulfilling. It's a world that's built around open communication, safety, clear and respected boundaries, and deep trust — all the qualities that are the main ingredients of true intimacy for me. Encounters in these worlds require constant communication between partners and constantly checking in with yourself to ask: What are your desires? Concerns? Boundaries? These are similar questions we need to ask ourselves on a daily basis when we sit down to eat.

I've entered a phase in my life where I feel

empowered sexually and I'm in a relationship with a man who loves and deeply respects me — plus, he knows his way around a knot or two. I feel incredibly blessed. And I've learned that when I feel safe, in my body and in the presence of my trustworthy partner, I can actually relax and surrender to pleasure. Now, with hindsight, I can honestly say that I am grateful for the beautiful, revelatory, transformative experiences that being rejected provided me. I finally feel like I'm becoming the sexually satisfied woman I was always meant to be.

WHY SEX IS SO CRAZY GOOD FOR YOU

When we trust our bodies and we engage in hot, mind-blowing sex, the benefits to our health are many. Having an active sex life helps you reach a healthy weight. Yes: having sex burns some calories, but more than that, it nourishes you both physiologically and emotionally in ways that naturally regulate and curb your appetite, while ramping up your metabolism and balancing your hormones. Sex replaces emotional eating with what you were likely truly craving: physical contact, comfort, connection. Sex also sharpens our senses and smooths out the rough edges of our moods by flooding us with happy, feel-good endorphins. It keeps us flexible, hones our muscles, and keeps our thyroid healthy. It's good for the heart and our circulation (ever notice how having great sex gives you a great complexion?). And that's not all. It's good for our oral health (all that kissing keeps our saliva flowing, which prevents tooth decay and boosts digestion), and it reduces pain and inflammation. It strengthens our immune system and helps us sleep better. Some researchers say it even fights cancer in men (studies show that men who ejaculate often are less prone to getting prostate cancer later in life). Having a healthy sex life is a cornerstone of having overall good health and I advise all of my clients, whether they're partnered up or not, to find their groove and get it on.

THE METABOLIC BENEFITS OF ORGASMS

When you climax, your body is flooded with beneficial hormones and your metabolic systems are enlivened and invigorated in incredible ways. Orgasms don't just blow your mind, they are packed with health benefits. Here are just a few: Having regular orgasms (at least once a week) helps your body grow healthy tissue, absorb nutrients, and balances your hormones. Women who have sex regularly report having more regular, less disruptive periods. Orgasms also boost fertility.

All sorts of beneficial hormones, including DHEA (which improves brain function, immune system responsiveness, and cellular growth and repair), estrogen, and oxytocin (a natural pain reliever and muscle relaxant), are released when you climax, and this is in part what gives you that healthy, post-lovemaking glow. Orgasms also stimulate the hypothalamus gland, which releases hormones that calm appetite, regulate body temperature, and keep all of your reproductive juices flowing and balanced. They massage the lymphatic system, too, which helps with the elimination of toxins and waste. There is no downside to feeling this good.

HOW PLEASURE BEGETS PLEASURE

Just as I was beginning to enjoy a more open, healthy sexual life, I also began to crave meat. It was as if my senses were awakening from a long, dark sleep, and both my body and my palate wanted more flavor, more nutrition, more satisfaction. It's funny to think about now, but I had a much easier time accepting that I wanted and needed kinky sex than I did breaking my veganism and eating meat. I had to work hard to overcome a sense of failure, a sense of disappointment — including feelings of shame and self-loathing, even — to get to the point where I could allow myself to feed my body what it was telling me it most needed and wanted.

I was discovering firsthand how deeply sex and food go hand in hand and how much judgment we need to shed in order to have a healthy relationship with both.

I recently supported a client, Donna, while she navigated her way out of a loveless, sexless marriage. When we talked she told me that her husband had rejected her so completely sexually that she felt like she was masturbating while she was on top of him in bed, desperately trying to engage him. She felt so humiliated and rejected that she went numb. She found that she wanted to sleep all the time, or at night, once the kids were in bed, she'd want to drink one, two, or three glasses of wine. She'd often sleep on the couch, just so she wouldn't have to sleep beside a man who no longer desired her. When we started working together, it was all about getting back to moderation in her diet, learning to listen to her body again and giving it what it needed to be awake and alert, not numb and heavy.

Donna worked hard to put the focus on herself and began working on her diet and her own general health. This move toward self-care dislodged in her what she described as an "itchiness," a sense of "pent-up energy," that she could no longer deny. It woke up her desires for a more fulfilling, love-filled life.

"At first, I told myself that I could stay in a loveless, sexless marriage, that it was the right thing to do, especially for the kids," she told me. "But as I took better care of my health, by eating well, resting, and just tuning into what my body was telling me it wanted, I couldn't deny my need for sex any longer. One night, when the kids were asleep and I was alone with my husband, I just started talking. I noticed that my hands, which had been crossed over my chest defensively, fell open and I relaxed as I told him, calmly and clearly, that I wanted to separate from him." She sat up and moved in closer to me. "Saying those words out loud was terrifying, but I immediately felt so much better. It felt good to be so open and honest. It felt good to speak up for myself and say what I really needed. From that moment on, I knew everything was going to be all right."

We talked about how being honest had

freed up so much energy for her. She told me that the next day, when she took her children to the museum, she actually felt like skipping on the sidewalk beside them. "I felt lighter. Freer. I had released something that was seriously weighing me down."

Within weeks of her talk with her husband, Donna also shed half a dozen pounds, without any extra effort on her part.

This is what healthy body love will do for you . . .

Even though Donna is still in the early phases of discovering who she wants to be in her next intimate relationship, the joyful sense of freedom and aliveness that I hear in her voice is infectious and inspiring.

Recently I took a field trip with Jessica Ann, my client whose mother freaked her out about being womanly. We went to one of my favorite sex shops in New York City called Babeland and I helped her pick out her first vibrator. When we walked into the store, I noticed that Jessica Ann kept looking around, as though she was waiting for a vice cop to jump out from behind the counter and arrest her. Instead, one of the staff approached us and gave us an excellent tutorial on the vast array of vibrators they had. Jessica Ann began to ask questions, and before long, she'd settled on a model that had some extra-special features. After we left, I felt like I was walking alongside a new woman, one who was excited about exploring her own sexuality. When we parted, I made her promise that she'd experiment with her new toy with a sense of playfulness and that she'd do her best to leave any shame or judgment outside of the play area. She promised me she would.

Female desire is a beautiful thing. We're here on this earth for such a breathtakingly short time and we lose out on too many opportunities to experience pleasure because we are so at odds with our bodies. In order to change this, we need to learn to love ourselves, from the inside out.

My client Lysa is such a great role model for not waiting for the perfect body, the perfect time, or the perfect guy to honor her sexual self. Though she's lost more than twenty-five pounds over the course of our work together, she threw herself into the world of dating before she'd lost more than just a few pounds. As she put it, "Once I began to really cultivate an intimate relationship with myself and even before I'd changed my eating habits, I began to crave more intimacy with others." Lysa told me that while she had once been all about saying no, now she was actively trying to say yes as often as felt right. She told me that she knew she was moving in the right direction when she felt nervous and excited about something. I asked her to give me an example and she shyly said, "I don't want to brag about the acrobat from the circus, but let's just say that my sex life is pretty adventurous and hot these days."

I say amen to that, because at the end of the day, at the end of this life, not one of us will ponder whether we were thin enough, quiet enough, meek enough, or "beautiful" enough, whatever that means. What we will take stock of is whether we really took a bite out of life, whether we loved enough, enjoyed enough, and gave and received as much pleasure as possible. This is what desire is all about: living life to its fullest.

It's what your body was born to do.

Watch bonus interviews on the relationship between sex, desire, and food at: www.AlexandraJamieson.com/WFDbonus

CHAPTER NINE:
REST AND REJUVENATION

Sleep is that golden chain that ties health
and our bodies together.
> — Thomas Dekker

Sleep is a spiritual practice.
> — Gabrielle Bernstein

Of all the things we crave in this life, the
one that we most need — yet we most often
deprive ourselves of — is sleep.

Sleep, as an essential life-giving activity,
gets very little respect in our culture. In fact,
it's often considered some kind of strange
badge of honor to boast (or complain)
about how little sleep one gets. Thomas Edison, the restless inventor, famously called
sleep a "criminal waste of time" and boasted
that he was able to get by on four or five
hours of sleep per night and work on average fifteen to twenty hours a day. Of course,
Edison also often neglected to mention that

he was a profligate nap taker, with cots tucked away in the corners of his labs, in his library, even in his garden. So though he may not have had much respect for sleep, he did need it, and he took it, albeit in unorthodox ways.

The publisher and political activist Arianna Huffington gave a talk not too long ago to a group of women in business about how she came to believe that sleep is the great key to success. But this wasn't always true for her. She only discovered the value of sleep after she passed out at work one day and hit her head so hard on her desk that she broke a bone in her cheek and needed stitches. After this "accident," which was caused by her own habit of overworking and undersleeping, she realized that sleep is an important, even feminist, issue, and she encouraged the women in the room to lead the revolution and get enough sleep. She went on the record as saying that it was time that women *did* "sleep their way to the top." She's a brilliant thought leader who is onto something vital, which is this: women need to make getting enough sleep a priority and a foundational heart habit so that they can live as passionately and as successfully as possible.

Since Edison's day, the amount of sleep

the average American is getting has dropped from roughly 8.5 hours a night to an average of 6.5 hours per night. That's a loss of two hours of shut-eye, or a decrease of almost 25 percent in only a hundred years. This represents a massive behavioral shift in a relatively short time. This plunge in our daily intake of sleep has taken a terrible toll on our health, our ability to function well in the workplace, and our ability to stay safe and even alive. Scientists are gathering eye-opening data that shows that there's just no prize to be won for staggering through life bleary-eyed and sleepy.

And if we wanted to blame someone for this, we would be justified to point at Mr. Edison, who is credited with creating the electric lightbulb, an invention that thrust us into a state of perpetual daylight. But living in a world of artificial lighting, despite its advantages, has pitted us against our own internal body clocks, which want — and need — us to sleep fully more than one-third of the time, which means, for most of us, a minimum of eight hours a night.

ALL LIVING BEINGS NEED SLEEP
Every living creature, including some single-celled organisms, needs to sleep. Each species, scientists are discovering, is born with

an internal "body clock" (in humans it is located at the base of the brain) that establishes the optimal sleep-wake cycle for that specific animal. We humans evolved near the equator, where a day is divided pretty neatly into two twelve-hour halves — one of daylight and one of darkness. Our body clocks are not coincidentally twenty-four-hour clocks that are wired to rise and be active with the sun and to settle and sleep at daylight's end.

Sleep historians know that long before there were electric lights or alarm clocks, people would retire at sundown, or roughly 8 p.m., and sleep soundly until about midnight. Then, from midnight to 2 a.m., they would be awake in what was considered a period of quiet meditation (this is when artists experienced creative calm, love was made, poems were written — all in the quiet dark and deep comfort of the bed). After this period of sweet semiwakefulness, another full four-hour block of deep sleep would be enjoyed, from roughly 2 a.m. to 6 a.m. Then, as the sun rose, the medieval or Renaissance woman would awake refreshed and ready to start her day. This pattern of split-sleep fell out of fashion toward the end of the seventeenth century with the advent of better lighting (candles became more affordable and no longer just a luxury of the wealthy; Paris began to light its streets, first with candles, then gas and oil lamps, and naturally other cities followed suit). This move toward artificial lighting coincided with the opening of the first cafés, and it became fashionable, even way back then, for the aristocracy to stay up late in these gathering places. So long before electric lighting became ubiquitous, we were already beginning to value industry — and being hopped up on caffeine — over getting enough rest.

Researchers have recently re-created this "divided" sleep pattern by sequestering sleep study subjects in dark, sleep-inducing habitats for up to fourteen hours at a time. After a period of adjustment, every sleep study participant reported feeling more fully awake and alert for the first time ever in their lives — even if they had woken for a period of time in the middle of the night. This is an important part of this research to mention, because many of us get panicky or anxious if we wake in the middle of the night. I hope that knowing that this may be hardwired into your brain will make you feel more at ease with these periods of semi-consciousness.

If you experience this middle-of-the-night

wakefulness, why not use the time as an opportunity to journal or just contemplate the beautiful things in your life. (In medieval times, this was an hour of deep prayer to commune with a higher power.) It is during this "twilight" hour between the two deep sleeps that vital stress-reducing hormones are released. This might explain why sleep experts encourage those of us who experience late-night insomnia not to panic, but instead to relax into it, to know that though you may be awake, this is actually a time (when the body is still but the mind is alert) when you develop your strongest defenses against stress. Maybe this is why the Dalai Lama has called sleep "the best meditation." Perhaps he understands that mindfulness, which is at the very heart of true wellness, can only be achieved when we are well rested.

What I love so much about sleep is not only how deeply mysterious it remains to us, but also how neuroscientists are beginning to understand, quite specifically, just how incredibly active the brain is during this time when the body becomes so still. We know that memory consolidation and learning take place when we sleep; this is why it's far more important to get a good night's sleep before taking a test than it is to stay up late and cram. The genes that are crucial to cellular restoration and rejuvenation are activated only at night when we are in the state known as sleep. Psychiatrists and circadian researchers are discovering that there are concrete connections between healthy sleep patterns and the prevention or effective treatment of serious mental illnesses. But beyond these important links, we're still intriguingly in the dark about so many health-building processes that take place during sleep.

Fortunately, however, we've been able to extrapolate some of the pluses by understanding the negative impact sleep deprivation has on health. Some experts even estimate that fully one-third of all health problems are directly linked to insufficient sleep. For instance, injuries caused by car accidents are certainly a serious health problem, and while we hear a lot about the risk of causing injury while driving drunk, most of us don't know that more than a hundred thousand car accidents in this country a year are attributed to tired drivers. When we are sleep deprived, we are all prone to "microsleeps," which are short, involuntary episodes of sleep that last anywhere from a fraction of a second to about thirty seconds. Microsleeps happen when we're overtired or doing something monotonous.

What's so frightening about microsleeps is that we don't know when one is coming on, nor can we recall one after it has happened. They are short periods of absolute dark, and they happen because having reached a certain threshold of tired, our brain just doesn't care if we're behind the wheel or not; if it must rest, it will rest — at great or even grave cost.

But this is just one of the health hazards we risk if we don't sleep enough. We are also prone to, among many other ailments: impaired immunity, stress-related illnesses (including heart disease, diabetes, and certain cancers), cognitive difficulties (poor memory, loss of creativity, poor judgment), and most noticeably, weight gain, especially in women.

SLEEPING TO STAY SLIM AND TRIM

The link between weight gain and insufficient sleep is, as it turns out, a well-studied one. Researchers who have tracked thousands of people have found that when subjects got fewer than seven hours of sleep, their risk of becoming obese rose nearly 30 percent. For those who got fewer than six hours of sleep, that risk rose to 50 percent.

In other words, if you're not sleeping enough, you will likely store and retain fat — despite all of your waking efforts to keep this from happening. This fact may explain why, in part, diets just don't work. If we're all busy chasing after the next work project, or the kids, or the next half marathon, at the expense of getting enough rest, we may find that we're compromising our health in ways that we're not even aware of.

This becomes even more of a risk for women because we need more sleep than men. Though researchers are not quite sure why, some speculate that it's because we use more of our brains during the day than men do, so we need to allow more time for our cortex (the language and memory part of the brain) to rest and recover. Whatever may be behind our need for more sleep, researchers have actually been able to quantify the difference: women, they've found, need on average roughly twenty minutes' more sleep than men each night, and if we don't get it, we are at risk for more depression, more inflammation, more pain, and more blood-clotting problems (which puts us at higher risk of stroke) than our male counterparts.

And, of course, our hormones play a role in whether or not we're able to sleep as restfully as we ought to as well.

There's a rhythm to our hormonal life, and usually the most dramatic shifts come early in our childbearing years, when the surge of fertility hormones can make the rolling arc of our monthly cycle more pronounced (the sleep hormone, melatonin, drops during our periods), and then again, at the end of our childbearing years, when menopause brings on the waning of those same hormonal surges and we experience a different kind of metabolic intensity while our bodies adjust to an entirely different hormonal distribution.

Of course, planted right in the middle of this hormonal spectrum are the years when we're either having children or building our careers or caring for our older parents or any combination of the three, and these responsibilities make getting a good night's sleep next to impossible for many of us.

When I first separated from my husband, I went through an awful period of disrupted sleep and it had a visible domino effect on my health. My skin broke out, I was prone to bursts of weepiness because my body was aching with exhaustion, I'd find myself dozing off at odd times, and I was crabby with my little boy. I knew that the only way through was to fight for a good night's sleep.

It took a lot of work (and some really sweet support from friends and loved ones who helped me manage the stress I was under), but I was able to hold the line and get back into a healthy sleep habit and keep the rest of my life humming along while I recovered emotionally.

CATE'S NEED FOR ZZZZS

I worked with one client, Cate, who gave birth to three kids in quick succession. She had two kids in diapers at the same time and a preschooler to chase after, and getting her children to sleep and nap and nurse meant that she was up at pretty much all hours of the day and night. When a well-meaning friend told her to take a nap when her children were napping, she didn't know whether to laugh or cry, because her kids, who were all at different developmental stages, did not have the same sleep needs or schedules.

Cate staggered through those early parenting years in a kind of zombie state, and when all of her children were finally planted in school and she was able to go back to work full time, she found that she still couldn't sleep through the night. When she saw her OB-GYN and mentioned her insomnia and how debilitating it had become, her doctor offered her a prescription for Ambien. Cate knew this wasn't the answer, and that's when she contacted me.

"I'm tired. I'm heavy. And I can't think straight." This is how she described her then-current state. In just those three short sentences, she put her finger on the three chief complaints of women who are sleep deprived. Her whole system was frayed and her exhaustion was creating a host of bad habits that exacerbated her fuzzy thinking and caused her to make poor food choices. These sleepy cravings prompted her body to pack on the pounds and drove her to rely on stimulants like coffee, energy drinks, and diet sodas to make it through her workday. I knew Cate was making the best choices she could given the red-flag signals her exhausted brain was sending to her, but even with all of these crutches, she would find herself weepy and down and, as she described it, feeling chronically disoriented. And she was! She was utterly out of sync with her internal body clock.

When the brain becomes as impaired from sleep deprivation as Cate's was, it sends out frantic SOS's to the body, begging it to take in any kind of energy source that will deliver the most immediate surge of useable fuel. Your exhausted brain actually asks for sugar, stimulants, and carbs, in a misguided attempt to get up and running again. Then a vicious cycle begins, where we cave in to our brain's need for support and we guzzle caffeine and eat sugary, carb-dense foods in order to function. Then at night we're so juiced on these substances that have been messing with our metabolic systems all day that we may turn to alcohol, or another kind of sedative, in an attempt to come down enough so we can lay our head on the pillow for a few hours.

When our systems are this out of whack, we have trouble falling into the deep restorative dream state our brains need in order to rest and rejuvenate. Then, when the alarm goes off, we pull ourselves out of an inadequate state of slumber, our bodies hungover from all of those stimulants, and we haul ourselves up and do it all over again. When we're in this broken-down, sleep-craving state, our brains go into desperate overdrive, producing too much ghrelin (the hunger hormone) and not enough leptin (the hormone that signals "full" to our brain), and drenches the bloodstream with stress hormones like cortisol. It's an awful place to be, as anyone who has ever experienced jet lag knows, and poor Cate was living under this kind of time-bent cloud all of the time. Despite the demands of her kids, her job, her husband, and all the rest, I had to find a way to help Cate break this unlivable cycle.

So we started with the basics.

I shared some statistics about sleep with Cate and she understood that she had to get a minimum of eight hours of sleep a night if she was ever going to feel better. My recommendation was that she put together at least a solid month of eight-hour nights so she could get a really clear sense of how this made her feel. We began by reverse-engineering her day. Since she had to be awake by 6:30 a.m. in order to get herself and her family up, fed, and out of the house on time, this meant that she had to be in bed and asleep by 10:30 p.m., latest.

Since most of us need at least fifteen minutes to fall asleep (you can tell someone is seriously sleep deprived if they fall asleep any quicker than this), I wanted Cate to be in her bed, lights out, by 10 p.m. This meant that she would have to forgo the usual two hours she spent between 10 p.m. and midnight hanging out with her husband, watching the news and *The Colbert Report,* and having a glass (or two) of wine. She felt a bit resentful about having to give up this "me" time, but she agreed to give it a try.

The first week was a challenge for Cate, because she could hear the muffled sound of the television in the other room and she could hear her children stirring in their beds. At first, she found it next to impossible to turn off her hypervigilant "mom" brain. She thought about everything that went undone that day — the laundry, things at work, something to pick up for one of the kids' school projects. She got so anxious that on the first night, she even popped out of bed to check her work email at 3 a.m.!

But three days into her quest for a full night's sleep, she actually fell asleep before 10:30 p.m. and woke up just before her alarm went off at 6:30. This was the first full eight hours of sleep Cate had gotten in more than six years. The next night the same thing happened, and the night after that, and then things started to change during the day for Cate, too.

Now when she awoke, she felt calm and rested enough that she didn't need to immediately chug a large mug of coffee. Instead, she took a few minutes to just sit and plan her day while she hydrated with a large glass (or two) of water. This simple act — having a glass of water upon waking — was, she told me, "the single greatest act of self-care I have taken in years." Because her brain was now less stressed and was producing less ghrelin, the hunger hormone, she was able to make healthier choices for breakfast.

Now, instead of eating the sugary cereal she'd become reliant upon (but that she'd been buying by telling herself that it was for her second-grade son), she had an egg (for protein) with some fresh fruit. She also took to packing her lunch, which consisted of a portion of whatever healthy dinner her husband (the cook in the family) had prepared the night before. She found that she no longer fixated on the candy machine humming away in her company's kitchen, or felt compelled to get a caramel coffee drink when the predictable afternoon slump hit. Instead, she allowed herself to close her office door, close the blinds, and nap for fifteen or twenty minutes when that 3 p.m. dip in energy came. This was the most subversive, radical thing she'd ever done at the office. And it felt great.

By the end of the month, Cate was sleeping eight hours a night as a rule. And, without any conscious attempt at dieting, she'd also lost seven of the thirty-five pounds she'd gained since she'd had her last child. But the weight loss was just a nice bonus. What was really important to Cate was that she felt less depressed, less stressed, and, as she put it, "finally able to operate heavy machinery" again. She felt like she was no longer being held hostage by the low brain-functioning state brought on by inadequate sleep. Now she felt alive again, and free to make important choices about how she would take care of herself going forward.

THE SUBLIME ART OF NAPPING

There's a growing awareness that napping can be incredibly beneficial to mental and physical performance. Once Arianna Huffington became aware of the benefits of sleep, she created "nap rooms" at the *Huffington Post* and employees there (as at other innovative companies, such as Google) are encouraged to dip into one of these dark, cool rooms during the day so they can recharge their brains. Some professional sports teams, including the Texas Rangers, set up quiet areas at ballparks so even when they're on the road, the players can work with their body clocks to stay sharp, alert, and quick. Studies show that the brain boost you get from taking a nap lasts anywhere from one to three hours.

Strategic napping is an art, and all it takes

is a little bit of planning and understanding what constitutes a great nap.

There's a pretty broad consensus that a short catnap, anywhere from twenty to thirty minutes, taken before 4 p.m., allows your brain the optimal amount of time to "defrag" and dump unwanted data so it's primed to make good decisions and to be most able to absorb important information postnap. It also won't hamper your ability to get a good night's sleep later on. Research has also found that sleeping too much longer than this may make you feel a little groggy and underwater, and it may also affect your ability to sleep through the night later on.

Naps are known to: increase on-the-job alertness by 100 percent; improve your gross motor skills and improve physical reactivity and accuracy; relieve pain, including headaches and migraines; boost creativity; lower your heart rate; aid in weight loss; improve your mood; lift your libido; and boost cellular health. And that's just a partial list.

In short, few people ever wake up from short naps feeling bad — they make us feel good and whole and happy. In fact, they work so well, I've committed to taking 3 p.m. "power hour" naps for twenty minutes at least three days a week, especially when I'm in a busy launch period. I've recommended to clients who drive to work but don't have a private office to take a thirty-minute break at that time and go close their eyes in their car, putting on a sleep mask or draping a coat over their eyes. And if you can't manage a nap, don't hesitate to just sit quietly, close your eyes, and drift for a few moments. It will do you a world of good.

THE BEAUTY OF SLEEP

Creating and maintaining a super-comfortable, supportive, and inviting place to sleep is one of the best things we can do for ourselves. In order to get a great night's sleep, you need to be able to rest in a cool, dark place that's free of all electronic devices (cell phones, tablets, laptops — all of it, even, some passionate sleep advocates would say, alarm clocks). I encourage my clients to invest in soft, organic cotton or bamboo bedding (I'd rather have a lushly made, comfortable bed than a pair of expensive designer shoes any day) and to keep the furnishings in their room minimal and as natural as possible. I recommend this because we are all exposed to enough environmental toxins when we're out and about in the world all day, and where we sleep should be as free of toxins as possible. (I spent more on my nontoxic, organic mattress than I did on my first car, but since I'm breathing inches from my mattress for a third of my life, I'd rather not inhale the toxic off-gassing fumes associated with "treated and fire-retardant" mattresses.)

I encouraged a client who suffered from some debilitating respiratory problems to change her mattress from a standard to a nontoxic, organic mattress and her breathing and allergy problems all but disappeared. She did some quick math and found that the mattress was saving her money on medications and trips to the doctor and would pay for itself in about a year. I encourage all of my clients to ask themselves if their mattress is really supporting them, and if it's not, to seriously think about investing in a better one.

I also recommend placing several specific houseplants in your bedroom. In their groundbreaking book *How to Grow Fresh Air,* NASA scientists discovered that different common houseplants absorb different toxins from the air, and breathe off pure oxygen at different times of day. The common snake plant (aka mother-in-law's tongue — what a terrible name and association!) provides oxygen at night, pumping what we need into the air while we sleep. Aloe vera plants absorb off-gassing, carcinogenic formaldehyde from new furniture and paint. Spider plants absorb toxic carbon monoxide that may leak from ovens or basements.

Long before you enter your sleep sanctuary, you need to be doing things throughout the day that will lead to the lovely unwinding your body and mind need in order for full relaxation and restoration to take place once you actually get into your bed. This means limiting the amount of caffeine and other stimulants you have and, if possible, not having any at all after lunch (except, of course, for a bite of dark chocolate if that's your true desire). It also means making sure you've gotten enough physical activity before the sun goes down and that you're feeling really balanced on the hunger scale when it's time to turn in.

I'm also a big believer in taking baths, turning off the television, and reading for an hour or so, playing a family board game quietly, drawing or journaling, or doing any activity that brings you a sense of calm and peace. It helps to lower the lights at least a half hour before bedtime, even in the bathroom while you're brushing your teeth, so that when you turn in, you are all about only sleep or lovemaking or cuddling and catching up. The eight or so hours you spend sleeping are the cornerstone of any healthy beauty regime. Toxins are drawn away from our cells while we sleep and cellular harmony is restored. There is nothing like rest to make a woman glow from within (except, of course, hot sex, which becomes even hotter when it's either followed or preceded by a great night's sleep).

A good night's sleep does so much good. It boosts your overall health and well-being by lessening any pain you might be experiencing, and reduces your risk of injury due to accidents; it helps your blood sugar and other endocrine systems stay steady and balanced; it reduces your risk for infection, boosts your immune system, helps you maintain a healthy weight, forestalls the onset of serious illnesses, like heart disease and cancer — the benefits of sleep are endless.

Sleeping well will also help your relationship with food. One of my favorite quotes about sleep is from David Gozal, MD, a sleep researcher at the University of Chicago. He calls sleep "the food of the brain," and it is! When we feed our brain the rest it craves, only then can it best support us, in both body and soul. When we're rested we are able to stay relaxed — especially regarding food. Then we can make wise food choices that will best support us. This is why sleep is so very delicious, and so desirable.

Chapter Ten:
Stepping into the Sun

Concentrating one hundred percent on our breathing, or on our steps, liberates us. We become a free person in just a few seconds, free to transform the habit energies of our ancestors.
— Thich Nhat Hanh

Just as our bodies crave sleep, they also crave being outside in the fresh air and sunlight, moving through the vibrant natural world into which we were born. I realize this seems obvious, but one of the chief complaints I hear from women is that they just don't get enough time outdoors. Most of us spend a lot of time indoors due to the demands placed on us by our families, our jobs, and our other responsibilities. Instead of roaming around, taking walks, observing our environment, or playing outdoors, most of us are stuck at a desk staring into the strangely hypnotic light of a computer screen; then, when the sun goes down, we sit and stare into the equally unnatural light of the television screen.

We're getting too much artificial light and not nearly enough daylight, which ironically is only made worse by our wanting to protect ourselves with long sleeves, hats, sunglasses, and sunscreen. But perhaps we're overdoing it. Instead of living outdoors, as our equatorial ancestors did, we've become indoor creatures, and consequently, we are now suffering from an epidemic of vitamin D deficiency.

WHY WE NEED VITAMIN D

Vitamin D is created in the body when the sun shines on our skin, but nearly 65 percent of us women aren't getting enough of it, as very few foods contain significant amounts of vitamin D. Foods that contain vitamin D are from animal sources, such as cold-water fatty fish (anchovies, sardines, and tuna) and egg yolks.

Vitamin D is added to many dairy products, especially milk, because it is crucial to the development and maintenance of strong bones, as it allows the absorption of calcium and phosphorous into bone cells. Back in the day, doctors discovered that the "sun cure" corrected bone malformations (known

285

as rickets) in children, so kids were sent outdoors at high noon to take in the maximum amount of sun. Later, sunshine was found to be a potent antidote to tuberculosis, and so sanatoriums popped up in natural settings that had great sun and fresh air.

Interestingly, these medical discoveries also led to the tanning craze that began in the early twentieth century and that only slowed a few years ago with the mad rush to block as much sun from our skin as possible. But many scientists believe we may have gone too far: the benefits of getting at least a half hour of direct sunlight a day must be weighed against the risks posed by not getting enough. That's because sunlight — which is converted to vitamin D in our bodies — protects us against heart disease, rheumatoid arthritis and other autoimmune diseases, high blood pressure, many cancers, chronic pain, and lots of other conditions that disproportionately affect women.

For instance, some studies indicate that as many as 70 percent of women who have breast cancer are vitamin D deficient. When breast cancer patients have been given D supplements, the rate of their cancer growth slowed demonstrably. This is just one piece of evidence that shows that vitamin D helps cells stay strong and healthy in the face of adversity, and because of this, it is believed to be helpful in preventing all cancers.

Vitamin D is the one vitamin we can't rely on our diet for, and though we can get it in supplement form, health experts agree that the best way to get it is by spending time outdoors, basking in the warming light of the sun. Vitamin D, as it's converted in the body, becomes a hormone that keeps many metabolic processes running smoothly, not the least of which is keeping us alert and our brains functioning efficiently.

Similarly, vitamin D boosts the ability of immune cells to fight off infection. Because of this, it's thought to lessen the devastation of autoimmune diseases ranging from thyroid disease to lupus by helping the immune system stay on target by boosting cell-signaling capabilities.

Having sufficient vitamin D helps boost our mood and memory, increases our ability to lose weight, and aids our ability to fight infection and ward off disease. Our bodies are brimming with vitamin D receptors — in the skin, the brain, the heart, our sex organs, our breasts — they are everywhere. They all draw in the building blocks that will become this fat-soluble hormone, which is so crucial to the proper functioning of more than a thousand genes and countless cellular processes.

So go ahead: step away from your desk and get out and stretch toward the sun.

SITTING IS THE NEW SMOKING

All that artificial lighting isn't the only drawback of being indoors all day; sitting for hours on end, hunched over a desk, has also become a huge health hazard.

Within the past year or so, some really frightening research has been reported that spells out just how dangerous sitting is for our health. On average, we spend more than nine hours a day sitting, while only seven hours sleeping. Think about that for a moment; that means we spend more than two-thirds of a day either on our backs or on our butts. And our bodies are not happy about this. Indeed, doctors consider spending over nine hours a day seated a "lethal" amount of sitting. Excessive sitting messes up our spine and our posture, causes our muscles to atrophy and become slack, contributes to foggy brain, and can bring on serious circulation problems that can adversely affect our feet and legs. And it's not just sitting at our desks that is so bad for us; research shows that slouching on the couch and adding just one hour of television a day increases the risk of death by 4 percent. Think about what just watching a two-hour movie will cost you — if you're not moving a lot to compensate for these sedentary spells.

Nilofer Merchant, a leadership visionary and inventor, has even declared that sitting is "the new smoking" because it is *two times* more likely to cause death than smoking. Knowing this makes me want to stop writing, get up out of this seat, and run for my life! Fortunately, we are getting the message, as evidenced by the growing popularity of standing desks, and some workers — especially writers who sit for crazy long hours — have even opted to invest in treadmill desks. These are innovations that are moving us in the right direction, but still, they're missing the main point, which is that we need to stand up, stretch, and give our brains a big old rest and let our limbs, our muscles, and our five senses take over for a while — and it's best to do this outside.

Merchant addressed this problem by switching from sit-down meetings to walking meetings, which aren't just meandering walks around the office; no, she takes her colleagues on long, somewhat strenuous hikes out of doors. She calculates that she's logging between twenty to thirty miles per week with an average of four walking meetings. She's found that walking alongside a colleague (rather than sitting face-to-face across a desk) has made her a better listener and a more creative problem solver. Plus, as someone who has never liked exercise because it takes her away from activities — including work — that she values more, she feels like she's not sacrificing one for another. She says that without fail, every time she and her walking companions finish one of these meetings, they feel joyful, which isn't an adjective usually used to describe a business meeting.

If you can't manage a full-blown hike or a nice chunk of time away from the office during the workday, you should still get up and move — at least once an hour, even if it just means standing and stretching. I encourage my clients to do some easy yoga stretches. Beth, a designer I work with, even does a modified fifteen-minute vinyasa sequence, every day without fail, three or four hours into her workday; she swears it keeps her sane and calm, even when the deadlines are looming. If you can, try to get in some simple hip openers, or even a handful of push-ups or jumping jacks, to get the heart rate up and the blood flowing. Even just getting up and taking a long stroll through the office for five minutes every hour helps mitigate the harm caused by sitting for long stretches. Plus, it will clear your head, making you more focused and productive. If you work in an office with an open floor plan, do some light stretching in the bathroom. You heard right: do some "bathroom aerobics" — press planks on the sink edge, a minute of wall sits, or a few deep squats, which also offer the added benefit of strengthening your pelvic floor muscles and helps with urinary incontinence. It might sound silly, but these little bursts of muscle activity get our blood flowing and our metabolisms firing.

KAREN'S STORY

I have a relatively new client named Karen, who is struggling to find a way to eat well without relying on prepackaged diet shakes to anchor her relationship to food. One of the first changes I asked her to make was to make sure she took at least a half hour — just thirty minutes — away from her desk for lunch each day. She has an extremely stressful job as an account manager, which is made worse by an overbearing boss who insists that her employees stay at their posts — even at lunchtime.

Because of this, Karen has become habituated to just guzzling a shake that she's brought in her handbag. (Her office doesn't even have a proper kitchen or break room, which seems downright inhumane to me.) She works through "lunch" and everything else until 7:30 p.m. each day.

We sat down recently and she told me that her boss was going to be away for a week and I said I thought this was a great opportunity to change this habit and leave her desk at lunch. My response seemed to frustrate Karen. She didn't want me to tell her that what she needed to do to improve her relationship with food was to get up and get out into the sunlight for a few minutes, she wanted me to tell her what she should be eating instead of the diet shake. But I refused to provide her with a menu or any specific food recommendations. Instead, I stayed focused on what I knew she needed most, which was to break the terrible habit she had of working through her lunch.

We soon found ourselves at a serious impasse, and we spent that hour together involved in a stubborn negotiation, with Karen insisting that she would only be able to take two lunch breaks away from her desk — but not more. When I pressed her on this, and reminded her that her boss wouldn't even be there to monitor her, she

got a little emotional. No one, it seems —
especially no one at her very rigid workplace
— had suggested to her that she deserved
any kind of a break at all, even a half hour,
which, if you ask me, is only half of a
reasonable lunch break. I gently kept ex-
plaining to her that by stepping away from
her desk and eating either outdoors or in
the lobby of her building (which had comfortable seating and massive windows), she
would be changing her relationship to food
in really important ways. I wanted her to
experience eating without doing it while she
was hunched over a computer screen, her
hands more busy with the keyboard than
with her food. I wanted her to get a psychic
break from her work, just as much as I
wanted her to get a physical break from her
workstation. It took a lot of repeating myself
for her to begin to understand that I was
asking her to take a stand for her self-care
that would actually shift her relationship
not just with food but with everything else,
too. I wanted her to understand that her
relationship with food would not change no
matter what she ate — if she kept eating it
the same way.

Even after an hour of discussing this, she
wasn't quite getting what I was saying, but I
knew something had shifted in her because

she was much less defensive and more vulnerable. When we stood up to leave, Karen asked if she could hug me before we parted. Of course! I gave her a deep, soulful squeeze and whispered in her ear: "I believe in you. You can do this." And I really hoped that she could, because stepping away from her work, for Karen, would be a radical leap into self-care and self-love. This was the direction in which she needed to move, in order to change her relationship to food, and to begin to identify what her soul was really craving.

WHY I DON'T EXERCISE

I hate the word "exercise." It reminds me of my middle-school gym class, which was one of the more traumatizing experiences of my life. I mean, who wants to be forced to try to climb a rope in front of a bunch of boys while wearing a bulky back brace? The experience left permanent scars on my psyche.

Exercise evokes work to me. And when I move, I don't want to be at work; I want to be at play. This may seem like semantic nitpicking, but please hear me out: I really love to move, I do! I just don't do well when moving my body is packaged as a kind of bitter medicine, as exercise often is.

I know that I'm not the only person who has purchased a pricey gym membership, only to set foot into that gym less frequently than I visit the dentist. I don't know if it was the intimidation factor (the two-story-tall posters of the überfit yet skinny models that draped the building probably didn't help) or the die-hard vibe that dozens of intense and mute souls pedaling or stepping or crunching their hearts out gave off, but whatever it was, going to the gym felt daunting and not at all appealing. So I let myself (and my credit card) off the hook and canceled my membership.

Don't get me wrong. I don't dislike being around other sweaty people: I love the awesome collective buzz you can get from a super-juicy yoga class or, even better, the rush you get from a no-holds-barred dance class, like the one I took with Grandma Fun. But these activities aren't exercise to me; they are play. And play is something that I indulge in as often as I possibly can.

Do you remember what it was like to let loose and play when you were a kid, preferably someplace far, far away from your parents, where you were pushing the boundaries of the known world, trying things that were risky, thrilling, and confidence building? Well, I sure do.

I remember back in Oregon spending long summer days on my badass bike, the one with the flowery banana seat. I'd tear around on that thing, handlebar streamers flying, my hair knotty, my knees scraped and churning, bumping through the woods and carving new dirt paths with my tribe of friends. We were wild and free and we would only go home when we were starving and it was too dark to see the ground.

If we weren't in the woods, we were pedaling over to the lake, our bathing suits on under our cutoffs, towels over our shoulders, flip-flops on our feet. We didn't wear helmets back then, and there was no entrance fee, so all we needed were two quarters for the day — one for a bag of popcorn and a Coke, the other for an hour of Ping-Pong or shuffleboard. We'd swim all day long, working hard to learn the skills we needed to graduate to the bigger pool, where there was a high-dive. This is the pool where all the teenagers hung out, but we didn't care; we just wanted to see who could make the biggest splash or cross the pool the fastest. We couldn't care less how we looked in our bathing suits. We all became strong and tan and confident. It was during those long days of freedom that I learned so many things, like resilience, trust, the value of failure and the gift of tenacity, and so much more. Being a wild child is where I first learned who I am and what I'm made of.

Boy do I yearn to feel that way now. And so I strive to, as often as I possibly can. And engaging in "exercise" just doesn't provide the wide-open forum I need to get there. So I have to look elsewhere for the kind of intense physical pleasure that lets me be free. And I've found most of my clients need and want this, too.

For me, the mainstay of my connection to this youthful exuberance has been having a bike. I realized when I was writing this book that I've always had a bike, since I was about four years old. I had one all through elementary school and middle school, high school and college. When I moved to San Francisco after I graduated, I brought my bike with me. It was a beat-up old mountain bike, which was perfect for urban exploration. Getting to know a new city by bike made me feel safe and less "alone" — it made me feel part of the whole scene.

When I left San Francisco for Lake Tahoe, the old bike came along, too. When winter settled in and I needed to get around, I'd walk or even hitchhike, which was common for young people in that mountain town. I didn't do this recklessly; I used the same smarts I'd developed as a kid to assess whoever was offering me a lift (usually it was someone I knew), and if it was a stranger and I got a bad vibe, I'd politely decline the ride.

Then, after culinary school in New York, I moved to Milan, Italy, for an internship as a sous chef, and I used my meager savings to buy a bicycle with a basket. I explored every inch of that glorious city by bike. The few times it rained and I took public transportation, I regretted it, as the buses I rode were full of morose passengers who kept their heads down and their mouths shut. Whereas when I was on my bike, I was usually whistling or singing or talking out loud to myself. And often, when I stopped, I'd find myself making friends with someone I'd just met. Riding my bike was so much more than exercise to me; it was a way of life. It was living. It was 100 percent pure, unadulterated vitality. And it still is.

Once I had my son, I added some new toys to my play repertoire. I spent a lot of time with my little guy in the great parks of New York City, often pushing him in a swing. After many years of doing this (and always wondering why the seats on the swings were so darn tiny and not big enough for my grown-up behind), I finally got smart and bought a hula hoop. Now, while my son swings his heart out, I stand nearby, swinging my hips and hula hooping like there's no tomorrow. When it's time to move on, we both leave tired and happy.

Another playtime activity I love is dancing. But I was never very good at formal dance classes; memorizing complex steps was hard for me, and I'd get frustrated at how out of sync my brain and feet were. But recently, one of my own coaches took me and a group of seventeen other ladies to a pole-dancing class in New York City called S-Factor. She told me to "wear something sexy and comfortable," so I showed up wearing yoga pants and a tank top.

The instructor led us into a large, darkened room that had a half dozen stripper poles anchored in the middle of it. We all sat around the periphery of the room and the teacher walked over to a switch on the wall and dimmed the lights even further. Then she put on some seriously sexy music and led us through a series of floor exercises that would become the moves we'd use on the poles. She encouraged us to use our voices and she'd walk among us, saying *Yes!* and *That's right!* and *Can you feel that?* in a way that was inviting and fun.

Before too long, I had lost all self-consciousness and was feeling loose and free, just like I had when I would be frolicking like a dolphin in the pool of my childhood. Next, she encouraged us to shimmy and crawl across the floor, if the spirit moved us. I realized that she'd created the perfect environment for shedding all judgment and joy-crushing inhibition. It was just dark enough, the music just loud enough, that my bitch brain was quieted and I became totally present. Then she came around to each of us in turn and led us over to a pole.

With me, she just nodded and said, "Okay, let's do this!" And I did: I found myself grooving with abandon, my hair flying, my eyes closed, my body moving in ways I never knew possible. When my turn was over, she simply invited me to go back to the outer edges of the room and to continue to have fun. When the class was over (it was an hour but it felt like the blink of an eye), I was drenched with sweat and had so many endorphins coursing through my veins that I felt like I was flying.

The collective vibe was incredible: I was in the midst of a group of incredibly hot, trusting, and alive women. It was an *amazing* experience — altogether very liberating. But mostly, it was just a total blast.

Since then, I've gone with my entrepreneurial mastermind group for some trampoline time, and even more boldly, some dodgeball (where we showed a team of teenage boys how it's done). I've also taken clients of mine to "Shrink Session" classes, which are an audacious blend of hip-hop, yoga, breathing, and spoken affirmations that leave you feeling calm and soothed and carefree. There is something about saying positive things out loud to yourself while moving in a room with others that really releases oxytocin, the "love" hormone, into your bloodstream. The experience is one of deep bonding and a sense of closeness I've never experienced in any other class before. Interestingly, oxytocin is a hormone that also inhibits cravings, and this may explain why we forget to eat when we fall in love.

Playing will do this to you. It will make you fall in love — with yourself. And when you love yourself, all sorts of great things can happen.

HOW PLAY SETS YOU FREE

There is much research currently being conducted that shows how good play is for us. Scientists are discovering that playing is a key activity needed to change habits because it takes us out of our comfort zone in ways that reset our attitude to life in affirmative, creative, and solution-oriented ways. In play, we're open to the unexpected, so we're open to new behaviors. Playing is a form of improvement; it takes us out of our heads and encourages our bodies to take the lead. Play is all about stepping into action, and action is what is needed to change any habit.

Think about it: What other activity begs us to surrender so wholeheartedly without our having any idea what the outcome will be? When a group of kids play hide-and-seek, no one can predict who will win, who will lose, or who may quit and go home. Play is all about taking the action and leaving the result behind — the thrill lies in the uncertainty of the outcome. This is how we need to approach eating and our cravings, too; we need to stay focused on how we feel — in the moment — and trust that if we take an action that will support our feeling good (relaxed, happy, stress-free, not overly full), then we will continue to feel good later on, too.

That's the great gift of play: the promise of feeling completely at ease in your own body and fully trusting that you will make decisions that support this state of ease and flow. Reconnecting with your "player" self is absolutely essential to getting real with your desires. By recalling when you were feeling your most fierce and free, you will tap into that part of yourself that transcends judgment and labels.

My client Erin had a really rough childhood and it was nearly impossible for her to connect with that sensation of freedom that only unbridled play unleashes in us. She felt frustrated that she couldn't conjure up that feeling, and I knew this was a sore spot for her, so we spent some time working on just acknowledging and processing the lack of joy she'd experienced as a kid. But one day . . . a breakthrough! Erin remembered going to the beach once with friends and how liberating it felt to run into the surf and play in the waves. I asked her to tell me about this memory with as much detail as possible, and she happily obliged.

"I just wanted to become a part of those waves. I loved having my arms over my head and jumping at just the right moment, so I would be lifted by the swell. I remember I had the biggest grin on my face. And I felt so giant, so a part of it all — the ocean, the sun, the sand. I remember getting home and loving that there was so much sand in my bathing suit. It was a sign that I was alive."

When you play, you connect with the most

authentic, elemental part of yourself, the place where your deepest desires live. You can only get there by letting go and letting yourself have fun. I encourage all of my clients to watch for opportunities to play. If you look around, they are everywhere — all you have to do is log onto YouTube and key in the words "flash mob" and you'll be on your way. Visit a dog park, or a playground, or a Zumba class at the local rec center. People manage to sneak in playtime in surprising places — you just need to look for them. Want to feel great and feel connected with your desires? Get out there and play.

Experience a Shrink Session with creator Erin Stutland and Alex at: www.AlexandraJamieson.com/WFDbonus

---

CHAPTER ELEVEN: BEGINNING ANEW WITH FOOD

First we eat, then we do everything else.
— MFK Fisher

One of the great benefits of quieting our bodies by pausing when a craving pops up, or by making a new choice instead of acting out of habit, or by detoxing and giving our body a chance to heal and rebalance, is that we get a much-needed break from our anxiousness around food. We get to take a deep breath and step back from all of it — the cravings, the overeating, the guilt, the shame, the sugar highs, the numbing with carbs — and just relax. Then, when we're ready, we can approach eating with calm and curious awareness.

To do this, we need to learn to trust ourselves around food. I mean really, really trust ourselves and believe that we are in control of our relationship with food — and not the other way around. To do this, we need to get out of our heads and away from our bitch brains and let our bodies take over. Our bodies are wise and they're fantastically self-healing — if only we let them. In order to stay strong and regenerative and high functioning, we need to give them the right kind of food.

LETTING YOUR BODY LEAD

Earlier in this book, I talked a lot about how deeply connected the mind and body are and how we either nourish or pollute both body and brain by what we eat. When we aren't eating for balance and calm, we're reinforcing those negative habit loops that keep us pinned down by our reliance on unhealthy eating patterns. You now know that when you take disruptive foods out of your diet, you will calm the body, which in turn calms the mind. From this place of balance, the mind is free to relax and step back and — if we let it — the body is able to take over and guide us toward the foods it really needs and desires.

It's important to really stress this point: our bodies are designed to run efficiently, smoothly, and from a state of aligned wellness. Our only job is to get out of the body's way so it can move toward health. One way we do this is to listen to the body's desire for the right kind of food.

To help my clients understand this point, I tell them to think about a powerful wild animal and how that animal eats. Whether your mind conjures up a grizzly bear sauntering into a running river to snatch a salmon, or a bird gathering seeds from a late-summer sunflower, each of these creatures, regardless of species, is naturally drawn to the foods that will make it feel the most whole and well. That grizzly bear doesn't wait for an "expert" bear to come out of the woods and indicate which fish contains more omega-3s, and the bird doesn't wait for its mother to tell it which seeds have the fewest carbs. Each individual, each soul, knows exactly what it needs — if it relaxes and trusts itself.

It is the same for us humans.

To find our way back to food, we need to *want* to be whole and to live honestly and wholeheartedly, and to do this, we need to trust ourselves, body and soul. We have to trust that our bodies know what they need — and that they will share this wisdom with us if we give them the space and peace they need to figure that out.

Learning to trust yourself takes time and patience and what Buddhists call a "beginner's mind," which to me means a willing-

307

ness not to judge, but to just begin again. If you eat something that doesn't agree with you or that doesn't make you feel so good, that's okay. Knowing what doesn't work for your body is crucial information to have! There are absolutely no mistakes to be made here. And there are no food lists or restrictions or forbidden foods or calories to count or portions to measure — there is none of that. There is just you, your very wise body, and your desire to feel good and confident in your skin. It is that simple.

WHY DO WE EAT?

On the most primal, essential levels, we eat in order to have enough energy to stay alive. Food is, first and foremost, our fuel. But of course it's not just that. It's also one of the greatest sources of pleasure available to us. Simply writing that last sentence actually made my taste buds come alive as a number of food sensory memories raced across my mind: the warm, yeasty smell when I walk past my favorite New York City pizzeria on a crisp fall day; or the first, fresh taste of a green smoothie after a night of great, deep sleep; or the smell and taste of the first ripe blackberry of the summer season when I look down and realize I'm barefoot for the first time in a long time. Oh, man! Food is such an endless source of pleasure — a pure, true, blissed-out, joyful kind of pleasure.

But there's a dark side to food, too — especially for women. For many of us, there are awful, toxic ingredients hidden in our food, like shame, guilt, and fear (which is stealthily sprinkled, like MSG, all over most foods). These are the emotional ingredients that call out to us with the same kind of ferocious irresistibility as the most highly engineered processed foods that light our brains up like pinball machines. We need to get honest with ourselves about the frequency yet falseness of these harmful, unhealthy emotional ingredients and decide, once and for all, that we're going to avoid eating foods that make us feel ill, unlovable, fat, undesirable — all of the demeaning, self-loathing ways we use food to sabotage our lives. From here on out, we are going to wake up each day and make a commitment to eat not only for fuel, but as an act of daily self-care. We are going to strive to eat for love and with love.

So beyond the need for life-sustaining fuel, we need to ask ourselves this very basic question: Why do I eat? I ask my clients this question and there's usually a bit of nervous laughter at first, followed by a profound few moments of silence. That's because most of us have never stopped to ask ourselves this question in a meaningful way.

Why do I eat? If you are honest with yourself, you may find you eat because you're lonely, or because you are stressed out, or sleep deprived, or sexually unfulfilled, or perhaps trying to fit in at some big social event when what you really need is to be home and quietly keeping your own company. The answer to this question is fluid because it changes all the time; sometimes it changes several times during a single day. To guide our eating with a loving hand, we need to get really clear on what's driving us to eat every time we put something into our mouths.

Now, don't get me wrong here: this is not about counting calories, or weighing and measuring portions, or following some rigid set of guidelines about what you can and cannot eat. In fact, what I'm suggesting is the *opposite* of all that. It's about taking the focus off of external influences and looking within. It's about checking in with yourself in a very strong, honest, yet kind way — so the bitch brain is absolutely banned from participating in this dialogue. Of course, she will weigh in from time to time, but the key is to acknowledge that negative voice and those toxic thoughts and then let them go. Then you can put your mental energy toward what really matters — mindfully choosing foods that will make you feel good about yourself.

You need to listen to yourself and get really clear about how you feel within your body and how you feel about yourself the moment before you take that first bite. This is fully aware eating, and practicing it will set you free.

Next we have to ask this question: How do I want this food to make me feel? In other words, what state are you hoping to achieve or move toward? Do you want to feel more alert? Do you want to just dull the hunger pangs in your tummy enough to keep doing whatever activity you are currently engaged in? Do you want to feel calm, centered, and at peace? Do you want to feel less weighed down and more energized? Or maybe you want to be hydrated, present, and connected? When you get clear on how you want food to make you feel, then you can step into the space where eating becomes infused with deep pleasure and great meaning. Because when you eat as an expression of self-awareness and self-care, eating becomes transformational: it becomes fun, it becomes a source of a different kind of satisfaction, and it becomes a source of life-giving love.

But Food Cannot Replace Relationships

We hear a lot of talk about "comfort foods" and we know that billions upon billions of dollars are made by companies that engineer the stuff. But the fact is, food cannot offer us the kind of comfort we're really craving. What food can do is either put stress on our bodies or calm them by providing nourishment and energy. But food cannot provide emotional support; only other humans can do this.

It's so important for all of us to remind ourselves of this fact whenever we're hit with that existential hunger for human connection that stops all of us in our tracks more often than we're comfortable acknowledging. This is a craving we all experience, regardless of our current relationship status. Being hungry for love or companionship is just another tender part of the human soul that the bitch brain loves to pick at, and this only heightens our anxieties about food.

Instead, we need to recognize when we are in the throes of uncomfortable emotions, and then, because we are not mistaking these complex feelings for physical hunger, we can make better food choices. Cultivating this awareness allows us to pause, however briefly, whenever we're triggered to react to a feeling by eating. Then we can take an action that will better satisfy this craving, such as calling a friend, taking a walk, or spending a night between the sheets with a lover.

It's important to remember that eating when we are caught up in anxiety or stress will not help our body reach a state of calm. Sure, food can put you into a coma and veil your anxiety by drugging your brain with sugar, but that deep peace you really crave isn't found at the bottom of the ice cream carton. When our feelings are highly charged, stepping away from food (especially alcohol or any of the Toxic Six) and getting engaged in something fun and pleasurable gives our hearts time to process and release those feelings. If we're too quick to rush to numb ourselves with food, our feelings get short-circuited and we collapse into an unhealthy loop of craving.

To break this cycle, we need to really digest whatever feelings we are having, and be okay with what we discover. It's important to stay away from the grocery store, the gas station minimart, and especially the fast-food drive-through when your feelings seem overwhelming. Instead, take a moment to check in with yourself. Put your hand on your belly, close your eyes, take a deep breath, and then ask yourself: What do I really need to feel the way I desire? What is my knowing body really asking for? Just by posing this question — the ultimate self-caring question — you will be further healing your relationship with food, without even taking a bite.

This is an area where detoxing can be a really great tool. When we consciously take certain foods out of our diet, we open space within ourselves that makes room for change. I use detoxing all the time in ways that are incredibly gentle and kind. This may be something as simple as deciding to not have alcohol for a month, or red meat for a week, or chocolate for today. What these choices give me is a sense of easy empowerment, a signal that I'm taking really good care of myself by constantly practicing awareness about how my body feels. Detoxing is like the bubble in the carpenter's level: it's a way to keep on cleansing so we can keep regaining our equilibrium.

EATING FOR BALANCE

One of my all-time favorite food quotes is from the inimitable Fran Lebowitz, who once said, "Food is an important part of a balanced diet." Amen to that! The challenge for most of us is getting clear about what qualifies as food and what doesn't and, once we've got a solid handle on that, learning to let our bodies tell us what they need, how much, and how often.

The person who illuminated the basics about modern food and who deftly cut through all the crazy diet chatter and got us refocused and talking about food and eating in a really sane and grown-up way is the writer Michael Pollan, author of *Omnivore's Dilemma*. Pollan's basic philosophy about food is neatly summed up in the Zen-like mantra "Eat food, not too much, mostly plants." With just seven short words, Pollan reminds us to be thoughtful about what and how we're eating, and he points directly at the best source of our food — the garden.

Mindfulness is the essential quality we need to bring to the tasks of gathering, preparing, and eating food. When we are aware of food in what I think of as a 360-degree way, we know that the decision we make when we're on one link of our own individual food chain will affect the choices we make further down that chain. For example, when I shop at the local farmer's market and load up on organic apples during the height of the season, this is the food we'll be snacking on at home. Conversely, if you are constantly dashing off to the convenience store, you are more likely to be munching on processed foods that aren't nearly as nutritious and healing as something you'd buy at a farm stand or even at the grocery store. In other words, where you shop for food and what you buy matter.

EAT TO BE REAL

When Pollan talks about food, he's talking about things that come from natural sources and not out of a box or can. He advises us not to eat anything "your great-grandmother wouldn't recognize as food." In other words, if something has a list of ingredients that you can't pronounce or are entirely unfamiliar with, it isn't food. If what you're reaching for is bright pink or electric blue? Not food. If it doesn't decay and eventually rot? Not food. Anything that's been pickled in a vat containing many mysterious chemicals? Definitely not food.

When you make a commitment to eat only real food, your options suddenly become very simple yet much more satisfying. It's

316

important to note that what I call real food is sometimes called whole food, or clean food. It can be certified organic, or pesticide-free, or hydroponically grown, or handed across the fence by your neighbor who fertilizes his garden with tea and coffee grounds. The point is that it didn't come from a factory and wasn't engineered in a lab, but rather came from nature.

Have you ever been to a really good farmer's market? If you have, you know how heady and satisfying walking through row after row of fresh fruits, vegetables, flowers, and nuts can be. I always feel very grounded and uplifted after a stroll through the market — and extremely grateful. But have you ever noticed how few types of food are actually there? A grocery store is filled with thousands of boxed, packaged, processed, and refined foodlike products. But not a farmer's market: it's just fruit and vegetables. Or, depending on where you live or what season it is, there may also be some honey, fresh eggs, maybe locally made cheeses and free-range meats. This is real food. It is simple yet profoundly packed with nutrition, flavor, texture, and scent. When you make the commitment to eat real food, you've taken a bold step — an important, meaningful action — into deeper self-care. Once you decide that you're going to do your best, one shopping expedition at a time, to stock your larder with the freshest local produce you can find, the noisiness of all those other food products will begin to quiet down.

Choose Foods That Support Your Desires

Shopping for food has gotten a bad rap. It's become too much of a chore. Most of us dread it, I believe, because we usually haven't added it to our calendar in any meaningful way. I've heard the advice to schedule time for exercise, just like you would an important business meeting, but I've never heard anyone suggest that we schedule time for food shopping with that same sense of making it a fun, fulfilling priority. Well, I'd like to suggest that you start doing just that.

It's important that you shop for food when you aren't tired, upset, or hungry. It's best to shop when you're feeling rested, calm, and alert — the same way you want to feel for that big meeting with your boss. Wear something that makes you feel good while shopping rather than rumpled sweats. Take a look around you. Are there open-air markets, gourmet shops, ethnic food stores,

CSAs (community-supported agriculture, where you give your money directly to the farmer at the beginning of the season in exchange for regular deliveries of fresh produce)? There are lots of great places to buy food that aren't grocery stores — but grocery stores are great, too! I mean, I love Whole Foods as much as the next woman. But the trick is to stay away from the stacks of cans and boxes and hug the peripheries where there are fresh items to pick up and smell, weigh, and select.

When you are out food shopping, regardless of where, ask yourself: What food will make me feel truly well? And then break that question down even further: What food will make me feel energetic, rested, or alert, yet at ease? Keep asking yourself these and other thoughtful questions about how you want to feel when you actually eat the food you're about to purchase, and bypass any food that you know is not going to help you reach that desired state.

Here's a great example of one of my clients learning how to do this. Pamela used to virtually live on frozen "lean" entrees. She worked incredibly hard at not one but two nearly full-time jobs because her greatest desire was to pay off her student loans. Since she was logging nearly seventy hours a week at work, the best she could do was stagger into the nearest grocery store when her refrigerator was empty. This was usually pretty late at night, and she'd shuffle over to the frozen-food case, exhausted and starving, grab a handful of whatever brand of frozen diet dinners were currently on sale, and throw them into her cart. Then she'd swipe her credit card, bag her food, drive home, and deposit those dinners into her freezer.

Night after night — and I mean night, because she'd usually eat after 9 p.m. — Pam would microwave one of those flash-frozen meals and gulp it down while standing at her kitchen counter. Then she'd fall into bed. She got no joy from eating. She took no pleasure from these foods. She would fall asleep feeling bloated and heavy and wake up feeling tired and hungry. She told me that she felt like she was poisoning herself, but she didn't know what else to do.

We started with her sticking to the same shopping schedule, but I told her she was forbidden from buying anything frozen. Instead, she had to buy her food fresh. Telling her this brought an immediate reaction: "There is no way in hell that I'm cooking at nine p.m." I told her I didn't want her to cook — I just wanted her to eat something that would nourish her body as well as her desires. I even volunteered to meet her at the market . . . before 11 p.m., since wild horses can't keep me up any later than that. She realized how serious I was then and told me that I didn't need to join her, but we did agree that I would be on the phone with her while she shopped.

When she walked into the market that night, she felt different; she had an accomplice now, someone who could explore food with her, and this helped her feel more engaged and less like she was doing just another lame chore. I told her to walk right to the produce section and tell me what they had in the bagged salad section. There were so many options! She decided on something called the Tuscan Spring Blend, a bag of organic greens and fresh herbs that was triple-washed and ready to eat. Before she left the produce section, I asked her to pick up two bananas, two apples, and two oranges.

Next we headed over to the nuts and dried fruit section of the store. There, she picked up a bag of pecan pieces and one of dried cranberries. Last stop was the dairy case, where she found the feta cheese. "You're done!" I said, and off she went to check out.

As she was walking to her car, she remarked, "Wow, that cost a lot less, and the bag is much lighter than usual! But you know what? I feel like I bought so much more food." And indeed she had.

We wrapped up our call by talking about how all she needed to do was put the salad greens in a bowl, sprinkle some nuts and cranberries on top, then toss it with a bit of feta, some salt, pepper, and a swirl of olive oil. She could even slice an apple or section an avocado and add that to her meal. All of this would take no more time than it took to microwave one of those frozen dinners. I told her to call me when she had a break the next day.

"Hi, Alex. First, thank you for shopping with me! My salad was delicious. I went to bed feeling really good and I woke up feeling refreshed for the first time in . . ."

I waited for her to reply.

"You know, I need to take this seriously."

"Take what seriously?" I asked.

"Me. My health. What I eat."

I knew then that Pamela was on her way. She was beginning to build an honest, meaningful relationship with food. As we continued to work together, she was able to find time to actually begin to cook, and she discovered something that most cooks know: cooking is relaxing. But first, she had to prepare her kitchen so she could enjoy putting her meals together as much as she would enjoy eating them.

THE KITCHEN AS A SACRED SPACE

I'm always a bit baffled when people spend huge sums of money remodeling a kitchen and then stock it with jars, cans, bags, boxes, and cartons of the same old unhealthy foods that cluttered up the old version of their kitchen. This is where being mindful saves us from our habits yet again. We spend so much time fantasizing about what we want our kitchens to look like: what kind of appliances we want, what kind of tile will make the best backsplash, and so on. But few of us take the time to visualize what we're going to put into that awesome new chef's oven or that gorgeous state-of-the-art stainless steel refrigerator.

You don't even need a kitchen out of *Architectural Digest* to realize that wherever you prepare food is a sacred space. And I know this firsthand from my first New York City kitchen. My partner and I had a tiny one-bedroom apartment in what was then the ungentrified East Village. It was a fifth-floor walk-up, and the shower and bathtub were basically in the kitchen, which had the smallest four-burner stove I've ever seen in my life. The oven was only big enough to hold a half-size cookie sheet, like a doll's oven. Next to the oven was the only sink in the apartment. There weren't even any counters. I was in culinary school then, and my boyfriend was a budding filmmaker, and we put our creative heads together and built shelving and hung hooks and made counters out of a sheet of stainless steel.

This space was where the magic happened. I fell madly in love with cooking in this kitchen and created and tested all of the recipes that appeared in my first book. I began to trust my relationship with real food here and learned to relax and let my body lead.

I was able to work in this thimble-sized space because it was impossible to clutter up. It was so tiny that I had to buy only what I was going to cook that day or it wouldn't fit into the mini-fridge we stashed in the corner of our four-hundred-square-foot home. When things are this simple, a universe of options seems to open up and really wonderful things can — and did — happen. This kitchen was my sacred space. I honored the work I did here by investing in one good knife, several good pots and pans, and a handful of key utensils. I strove to make everything with the freshest ingredients I could find, and I found delight in blending tastes and fragrances — I was proud of what I created there. Being in the kitchen, for me, is being home.

DETOX YOUR KITCHEN

When it comes to helping my clients (and family and friends) get better situated in their kitchens, I am as no-nonsense as the Supernanny and as ruthless as Simon Cowell. Nothing gets me more worked up than a kitchen cupboard teeming with expiration dates! I have been known to barely glance at the back of a box, because I can tell, when the list of ingredients runs longer than a line or two, that whatever's inside has to go. Michael Pollan is with me on this one: he recommends staying away from foods that contain more than five ingredients, max. I've had to work hard to not just push a client aside and sweep whole shelves of food into garbage bags, but the truth is, this kind of cleaning is something people have to do for themselves.

I remember working with one woman, Vivian, who was as gung ho as I was about cleaning out her kitchen. "This is like an episode of *Hoarders* — but with food!" she said gleefully. But once we got started, she had trouble letting things go, even if she knew they weren't serving her. We hit this wall of resistance hard when we came upon a stockpile of boxed brownie mix at the back of a deep shelf. These had not yet expired, so they went into the pile of canned and boxed goods that Vivian would bring to the local food bank once our cleanup was done.

I asked her why she felt like it was hard to give these up, even though she'd given up sugar and processed baked goods months before. "They remind me of my mother," she said. Then she told me that her mother had baked this same brand of brownies for her when she was a little girl, whenever she was sick. Her mother had died a few years before, and she realized that having this box — even just to look at — made her feel close to her mom.

"How about you take a picture of the box with your cell phone?" I suggested. Vivian loved this idea — she snapped a picture of the box, then put it and the others into the donation pile. In no time at all, we had cleaned out her cupboards, wiped them down, and we even managed to clean out her fridge, too, jettisoning the contents of partially filled bottles and jars that were hiding in plain sight on the inside of the door. While we worked, I learned so much about

Vivian as she regaled me with really juicy bits of her food history. As it turned out, this kitchen cleansing also turned out to be a great bonding experience for us. The best part? Now that Vivian's kitchen was clean and unburdened, she could relax into it and get busy.

DISCOVERING THE JOY OF COOKING

People who love to eat are always the best people.

— Julia Child

When I was a child, my mother loved to watch Julia Child on TV, not only because she'd learn a thing or two about cooking, but because Julia was always so stoked to be behind her counter. Her voice just rippled with pleasure and her sense of humor was surprising, even bawdy. There was another TV chef back then, too, a guy named the Galloping Gourmet, who pranced around his kitchen sloshing an always-full glass of wine. By the end of many episodes, he was clearly tipsy and usually cackling with delight.

Compare these early cooking shows to the ones that are popular now. Most of them are competitions, where the contestants have to prepare something insanely complex with crazy, hard-to-find ingredients, while a sadistic celebrity chef berates their every effort. I mean, where is Julia, who famously dropped a chicken on the floor, picked it up, and kept right on going, when you need her? Cooking isn't torture. Or at least it shouldn't be. But a lot of people view it that way, which doesn't make a lot of sense, given how much we all love to eat.

Then there's the rationale that you are too busy and cooking just seems like such a hassle: it's hard, takes time, it's messy . . . I hear you. It can be all of those things. But it's also an amazingly energizing, desire-meeting activity of the highest order. When we cook, we are engaged in a kind of magic where we conjure up something delicious and nutritious and healing. From simple things, a universe of possibility and pleasure is born — especially when you discover that you actually like spending time in the kitchen. Besides, cooking is the most essential of life skills; if you can cook, you always have meaningful work, you are always able to express love and gratitude in practical ways, and you can always nurture yourself and others in a delicious fashion.

Cooking is also an art that blossoms with practice and time. If you play an instrument or engage in another form of art, you know what I mean: once you have the basics down and your confidence begins to build, you step into the realm of improvisation and jazz, and when this happens, cooking becomes singular, a unique expression of who you are as a person.

When we cook for ourselves and others, we bring a level of devotion and attention to the task that infuses whatever we prepare with integrity. That's because when we cook — if we really give ourselves up to it — we are fully present and aware of every step in the process. Being in the kitchen, working alone or alongside someone, is a form of devotion. It's a gesture of praise for good ingredients, good tools, and the good people we will feed. When I'm really in this zone, I feel like a goddess, and I love that feeling.

I find that I most easily achieve a state of flow in the kitchen. I can't really describe it, but when I'm chopping beautiful, fresh ingredients, or gently stirring a pot, my hands and heart meet in a deeply satisfying way that is only rivaled by lovemaking for me. I enter a sweet, empowering zone when I'm lost in a recipe, and when I step out of the safe structure a recipe provides and I invent something new, I experience a sense of accomplishment that's hard to beat. It's thrilling. It's enlivening. It's powerful. And I want all of my clients to experience this joy firsthand.

One of the things I love most about cooking is that it is an enemy of perfection. Trying to be "perfect" is a crazy goal that's hobbled and distracted women for far too long. Cooking isn't perfect, it's like life: sometimes you burn it up, sometimes it goes flat; sometimes it's too spicy, other times it's too bland. Preparing food is a lot like building a sand castle, too: you labor and admire — and then, poof! It's gone.

But when you cook well, the memories of a good meal, or a great apple, or a sublime bite of chocolate get stored in your cells. This is when food becomes the body; it becomes a part of your cellular memory and informs who you are.

REVEREND DEBI

I have a client, the lovely, effervescent Reverend Debi, who is a missionary with a huge heart. She's also been suffering from digestive disorders for many years. By the time I met her, she'd had much of her lower intestine removed and her digestive system was extremely low functioning and hypersensitive. Debi wanted me to help her figure out what foods she could tolerate that would provide her with the nutrition she so desperately needed.

We slowly introduced things like whole grains soaked in water overnight (this removes the acidity from them) and grass-fed beef, liver, and wild salmon for the healthy fats and dense nutrient value they had. I taught Debi how to make vibrant green smoothies with bok choy, peas, apples, and other nutritious foods that would be easy on her embattled system. Debi was an eager student and she loved how these new food choices made her feel. But what she loved most was how much she was enjoying preparing these foods in her new favorite room, her kitchen.

"I've really taken your advice to heart about approaching food with nonjudgment and healing intentions," she told me. "Now I really believe that food is on my side. Because of this, my cutting board is now like an altar to me, a place where I do sacred work. I want to honor my food, so I've thrown out all the old plastic containers that were cluttering up the space and I've replaced them with clean glass. Anything that doesn't enhance the beauty of what I'm making, I've gotten rid of."

We talked together about how she was actually eating the food she prepared, and she told me that though she lived alone, she set a gorgeous table for herself each night, lit a candle, said a prayer, and savored her food.

"That's my self-care time, Alex. Dinner is when I get to celebrate me, by putting really wholesome, healthy food into my body."

Since transforming her diet and her relationship with food, she'd become more social, too, carrying the things she now knew about how various foods affected her out into the wider world. She felt entitled to say no to foods (even the fried dishes she'd grown up on and loved), to set clear boundaries for herself around food. This energized her tremendously and she began to throw small dinner parties of her own at her lovely, regal dining room table.

"Breaking bread with those you love is a beautiful thing," she said to me recently. "It's an affirmation of life." Debi understood what I want all women to know, which is that how we feed ourselves is an outward expression of how we feel about ourselves. We have to believe that we're deserving of the deep nourishment only healthy, real food provides, and that we're worthy of creating it and sharing it with ourselves and those we love.

Learning to find the foods that best support you, learning to prepare them, and relaxing and detoxing from the rest of the world while you enjoy your meals — all of these skills take time to learn and build. It's not a linear process and there is no goal to reach. There's just you, food, and your desire to take excellent care of yourself.

When you approach food with gratitude and curiosity, while listening deeply to your body, you will discover a way of eating that will inspire and sustain you.

For craving-worthy recipes and kitchen detox strategies, visit: **www.AlexandraJamieson.com/ WFDbonus**

CHAPTER TWELVE:
HOW DESIRE WILL
SET YOU FREE

Our deepest fear is not that we are inadequate. Our deepest fear is that we are powerful beyond measure. It is our light, not our darkness, that most frightens us. We ask ourselves: Who am I to be brilliant, gorgeous, talented, fabulous? Actually, who are you not to be?
— Marianne Williamson

BUT FIRST, THERE IS FEAR

The first time I read this quote from Marianne Williamson (which is often attributed to Nelson Mandela, another hero of mine who never gave up on his desire for freedom), a jolt of recognition shot through me, because I have experienced firsthand just how terrifying it can be to step into your truth. Identifying and taking action on our desires takes guts; you really have to decide that taking care of yourself matters more to you than how others might react.

For me, this first became evident when I really began to embrace and honor my sexuality. This period of wonderful erotic awakening took place after my painful and traumatic divorce. The end of my marriage left me feeling unsure about my desirability as a partner and my right to be a sexually fulfilled woman. Despite feeling afraid of intimacy and distrusting of men, I got back out there and started dating, and I discovered that I was able to examine and explore my sexual needs by flirting, kissing, cuddling, and, when my confidence grew and the conditions felt right, engaging in some really glorious, hot, and healing sexual intimacy with new partners. I began to understand what I needed to feel safe enough to trust my sexual body, to trust my sexual desires, and to identify what qualities I really needed in a sexual partner.

But interestingly, as my sexual confidence grew, the men I was dating grew suspicious and distrusting. They wanted constant reassurance from me that I found them desirable, and the last few men I dated before I met my current partner even wanted me to guarantee that I wouldn't share my sexual self with any other men. These guys wanted me to be monogamous with them, even though I was clear that casual dating was my current reality. When I refused to agree to this, several men stopped returning my phone calls, and others reacted initially with judgment. But then they realized that they really didn't have a right to judge me (they barely knew me!), so those relationships simply ended without much drama. In the end, those partners and I just agreed to disagree about how we dealt with our sexuality and bodies.

I had stepped into the world of healthy sexual desire, where self-fulfillment became paramount. This wasn't about misusing or harming others — this was about discovering what I wanted and learning how to ask for it. It was about healthy boundaries, mutual consent, and lusty playfulness and joy. It was about finding satisfaction within myself, and from this place of acknowledged desire, I was able to please and satisfy others. Honoring desire was, I began to learn, what healthy sexual intimacy is all about.

Once I settled into my relationship with Bob, my handsome boyfriend, another desire that I'd been fighting and tamping down finally pushed its way out of my head and into my body, demanding that it be met. For a full two years, my body had been craving meat, eggs, and other animal products. I had, as you now know, been vegan for more than a decade by then, and I'd built my career as a vegan chef and a holistic health counselor who was open about her veganism (though interestingly, most of my clients were not vegan, and I happily supported them to find their best diets). But when my body started to break down, before I could give it what it really needed, I was so crippled by shame and guilt that I hid my cravings from everyone, including my partner and son.

You see, I was afraid of disappointing people; of somehow letting down my tribe of fellow health warriors, or my clients, or anyone who found inspiration from my work while being vegan. But more than that, I was afraid of being judged; I was afraid that making this kind of change would somehow make me seem less loving, or less credible, or less trustworthy, so I kept my desires hidden. It wasn't until I began to realize how harmful these fears were that I was able to finally own and honor these desires — because I knew deep down that honoring my desire, giving my body what it was craving and calling out for, would actually make me more trustworthy, more truthful, more authentic, and much more reliable to everyone around me.

So I began to eat free-range eggs, locally sourced, grass-fed meats, and wild fish, in an effort to get more healthy omega-3 fatty acids and avoid the dangers of factory-farmed animal products like antibiotic-resistant germs. But still, I didn't tell anyone, not even my closest colleagues. And that's because in my gut, I knew that I would be criticized and ostracized for changing my life by changing my diet.

But I wasn't at all prepared for what actually happened.

CHANGE IS SCARY, BUT A POWERFUL WOMAN IS SCARIER

When I came out as no longer being vegan, old friends stopped talking to me, longtime colleagues renounced me, and I was flooded with messages via social media that were way beyond anything I'd ever experienced in my life (before or since) in terms of how vicious and hateful they were. Some ultra-political vegans even wished me dead! I was not prepared for this onslaught and it really undid me emotionally. I cried a lot those first few days, sobbed under the covers in my bed — that's how wounding that initial response was.

But then an email came in praising me for being so brave. Then another, and another . . . I started to get texts and emails and messages on Twitter and on my Facebook page, thanking me for having the courage to advocate for myself and to speak my truth — and, especially, to stand tall in the face of so much criticism. The tidal wave of support that began to swell after the haters got in their vicious jibes lifted me up and out of the fear and doubt that had me pinned down, and soon I found that the effect of being so honest and transparent was that I felt lighter, calmer, and more energized. In short, I discovered that being honest had set me free. And this freedom felt good. Very good.

Since that coming-out experience, I've had other vegan "celebrities" confide to me that they had also needed to add meat back into their diets, but they weren't yet ready to share this news with their readers and clients. The fear was that they'd lose their businesses, lose their credibility, lose their community. I understood this reticence all too well; it took me a full two years from initial craving to making a formal announcement, via a video I shared on YouTube, to come clean about my evolving diet. It took me a long time to find my voice and the guts to speak up for myself. Reading Brené Brown's powerful work *Daring Greatly* helped me understand that vulnerability is a strength, not a weakness. When I finally came clean, it was the best thing I'd ever done for myself.

I share this with you so that you understand that giving yourself *time* is essential when you are easing into alignment with your desires. It's crucial to be kind to yourself, and part of this generosity has to be expressed by not rushing yourself. There is no timeline or "right way" for this process to unfold within you; it is as individual as you are, and part of the deep self-liberation that comes with finding your own way to express your deepest, most heartfelt desires is born in this time of great patience. Giving yourself the time and space you need to get behind your own game plan is key to making any great, significant change. In my private practice, I find that my clients are really hard on themselves about time; they tend to beat themselves up if they don't get it right quickly. I have to assure them that taking things slow and making mistakes is the best way to ensure long-lasting change that feels good.

Taking ownership of your desires is the ultimate hero's journey. Strong, independent women through the ages have been leading us by example, showing us how to live with integrity and not deny that which is most primal, essential, and natural to us. But there has always been a cost to us, when we truly step into our desires. Our cravings and desires can be perceived as threatening, rather than as life-giving.

IT ALL BEGAN WITH EVE

We need look no further than the Bible and the story of Adam and Eve to see how the desires of women have been labeled as dangerous or wrong. All Eve did was reach out for an apple, for some simple, natural nourishment and knowledge. All she wanted was to be fulfilled. She wanted to be energized by experiencing. And this craving led her to a desire to feed herself something wholesome, fresh, and real. I mean, c'mon: What is objectionable about that? As it turns out, Eve reaching for that apple was a radical act of self-care, one that the world just wasn't ready for yet. Her simple gesture was portrayed as threatening the patriarchal power of God at the time the Bible was written, and for whatever reason, those in power felt the need to equate Eve's natural and healthy hunger and passion with the concept of "sin." In other words, Eve was made to feel wrong for wanting to take good care of herself. Sound familiar?

At that moment of hunger, Eve felt so good and at ease in her own skin that she approached that tree as naked as a baby. It's worth noting that her lover and sexual partner, Adam, was also nude, and neither of them seemed to have any issues like body shame. Adam was clearly an enlightened guy, because he supported Eve in her desire, and like her, he wanted a taste of that ripe, delicious apple, too. We've spent the last several thousand years trying to get back to that state of innocent, open, naked, and raw freedom. To get back into the garden.

When you look at the story of Adam and Eve from this perspective, it's almost as though the big, industrialized food machines got their hands on them and pushed them away from the whole foods and healthy sex they needed to stay free in their bodies. I can't help but love Eve because she was an early badass feminist. She was the original poster girl for claiming real, nourishing pleasure.

I wish I could say that things have really evolved for us since Eve's story was first penned, but we're just getting to the point where a woman who expresses her deepest desires — whether they involve food, sex, work, family, or play — is perhaps not immediately judged or criticized. But we still have a long way to go. When a woman expresses her desires, it still too often causes some serious blowback. And too often, the harshest judgment comes from other women! I want this to stop. And it stops when each one of us makes a commitment to stop judging ourselves and others so harshly. But until we get there, just taking a step into desire, into our purest natural state, is still for women both individually and collectively a very radical, necessary first step.

I'm convinced that the more we support each other in shamelessly discovering and declaring our desires, the easier it will become for all of us, and the more our desires will be met. When we build on this idea of being truly mutually supportive, really beautiful things will begin to happen everywhere. Feminine power is the greatest untapped natural resource we've got, and every time a woman realizes her desire, that energy flows into and enhances the world. Just imagine the power that would be unleashed if we stopped focusing on the number on the scale or wondering if we are good enough or worthy enough? Stepping into desire helps us surpass these limitations and launch into action.

You Don't Have to Do It Alone

In fact, I don't want you to do it alone. Having the right kind of loving support around you while you learn to identify and express your desires is crucial. Albert Einstein once asked his lab partner, Niels Bohr, if he believed the moon was still there if nobody saw it. He was illustrating the point that something can exist even if we don't see it. I agree with this . . . but I still want to see that big bright ball of moon! That old moon makes the tides turn in sync with the spinning world; it regulates the rhythms of our hormones; and when it's full, it's a great metaphor for what happens when female desire is realized. Because whenever a woman finds the courage to take action on a desire, the rest of the world benefits from this act of bravery, however quiet, however private, it may be. Every time one of us asks for a raise, ends a bad marriage, or commits to eating only whole and healthy foods; every time one of us takes an action that will improve our health and well-being *and* our happiness, we not only improve the health and well-being of everyone else on the planet, but by our example, we give other women the *permission* they need to satisfy their craving to live a more meaning-ful, vibrant life.

Human beings are tribal creatures. We are hardwired to be in communion with one another, as families, partners, communities, companies. We're meant to lift each other up, to help each other reach our dreams. This is what fuels desire: the wish to be vital, contributing, cherished members of our communities. We are all able to be our best, to become our best, when we're buoyed by genuine, loving support from those around us.

But sometimes this means we have to do some legwork in order to find our tribe. We may have to see a therapist, hire a coach, join a new gym, find a mentor, or talk to the mothers on the other side of the playground in order to find people who are willing to look at us with fresh eyes and open minds. Or sometimes we simply have to risk being seen anew by those who already know and love us; you may have to summon the courage to have the difficult conversation, to tell someone you love that you're not getting the kind of support you need. These conversations, I've found in my own life, shift the energy around us in ways that are always ultimately beneficial, though when we're having them, they may cause us, or the person we're communicating with, to feel a bit uncomfortable. We need to find people who will validate our desires, but who won't feel compelled to interfere with our ability to achieve them.

We love each other best when we stand most firmly on our own, independent and strong, and when we stand lovingly separate. In order for any of our desires to become real, they need space as well as time. They need room to germinate (desire begins as a wish, a prayer, an idea, a spark of creativity) and grow, and this can only take place within the body and soul of a woman who feels entitled to grow her desires without impediment. If we crowd her, or badger her, or doubt her, we run the risk of casting our own shadows on these budding desires and not giving them full access to the sunlight they need so their potential can really bloom.

So though we need to know that we're loved, we also cannot expect others to meet our desires for us; they are ours to own, ours to express, and ours to savor. I run into this kind of transference from time to time with clients who begin their work with me full of lots of motivation and energy. But for some inexplicable reason, at some point in the process of our working together, they begin (unconsciously) to project all of their expectations onto me and then they stop taking action. I watch helplessly as they subtly stop taking care of themselves. Instead, they begin to wait. They wait for me to take an action or say the right combination of things — anything that will help them to move closer to reaching their own goals.

I bumped up against this with my client Karen, the woman who wanted to know how to eat better, yet who refused to stand up for her right to take daily thirty-minute lunch breaks at work. It was so clear to me that she really wanted to have a good relationship with her body and a healthy one to food, but she had ingested and absorbed all the "no's" of those around her — especially her very domineering boss.

Early in our relationship, I knew to expect some resistance, but as our work together progressed and Karen became unwilling to even try what I suggested, I honestly contemplated ending our relationship. This is something I rarely do, but I've learned that if someone isn't willing to take real, tangible action steps to express her desire, nothing I can say or do will change that. In other words, if my clients don't make the deep commitment to themselves to take the difficult steps to break bad habits and to build new ones, there isn't a lot I can do to help them.

When I've hit this point with clients, I've been known to lay it on the line — without judgment or reproach: I just express as clearly as I can that I'm not seeing accountable action on their part. I then follow up by saying that I'm here, and that if they need more time to get clear on their goals, that's okay. By creating space for clients to find their way, to have their own "come to Jesus" conversation with themselves, I'm actually doing my job. And as I write this, I'm happy to say I haven't lost a client yet.

Karen didn't want to challenge her boss's no-lunch policy; instead, she wanted me to count calories with her, or create meal plans for her — in other words, to give her an "out" for what she really needed to do. But the more she tried to dodge her responsibility in meeting her goals, the more I held the line; I knew she was coachable — she just needed to reach deep down and find that part of her that really believed she was worth deep self-care.

Desire doesn't do well when it's handed over to others. I believe this is why so many diets fail. By design, we're set up to look to another, an "expert," a "guru" to fix us. But this kind of looking outside of ourselves for the answers cannot work where authentic desire is concerned. Instead, we must turn our hope inward and really get comfortable and grounded in our own good counsel. We need to listen to our cravings and hear the wisdom behind their facade of anxious longing. Inside of each of us is the motivation that will propel us toward realizing our desires, and we need to really grasp that no one else can provide this motivation.

I'm not saying that others can't provide the essential emotional, financial, physical, or social support we need in order to marshal our motivation in the most enlivening way — bringing our desires forth into the world requires finding a receptive and appreciative audience — but we cannot expect the audience to put on the play. We have to do that for ourselves. And in order to do this well, we need to unleash our creativity.

Esther Perel, the brilliant psychologist who is an expert on love, eroticism, and relationships, talks about how a "crisis of desire is often a crisis of imagination." She understands that though we may be committed (to a partner, and to extend her idea, to eating healthy foods, sleeping more, working more compassionately), if we're not allowed room for exploration and inquiry, our desire can die.

This brings up some hard truths about desire. Desire and habit are seemingly incompatible. That's because it feels like there is no imagination in habit: our brains are on autopilot when we're engaged in anything we do automatically, so there is no element of surprise, no element of discovery, and desire is above all about actively seeking out the new — even the new in someone we've known for ages, or in doing something as seemingly mundane as feeding ourselves. But I see a freedom within the framework of supportive habits. Rather than being forced to create a work of art on a blank canvas, many artists appreciate and flourish with a design concept or subject to play with.

Because desire operates beyond habit, it also invites failure, which most of us strive to avoid at all costs. I call my life a series of successful failures. In the real, grown-up world, our desires aren't always met, but that doesn't mean they go away; when we hit resistance or a dead end in our pursuit of our dreams and desires, this is just the universe indicating that we need to adjust course. Women who understand this accept that failure and rejection are experiences fundamental to achieving what they desire, so they approach life's challenges with a sense of adventure that outweighs their fear of failure.

In other words, when we begin to grasp that failure is a stepping-stone to defining and achieving our desires, we move closer to taking meaningful action. Accepting failure as a possible outcome, without harsh self-judgment, builds expectation and anticipation. As a writer friend once said to me about what it's like to submit stories for publication: "I gather each rejection as though it were a single red rose. When I have a giant bunch of them, like two dozen or so, I know I'm getting really close to a yes." As she told me this, I saw her in my mind's eye, standing there, a smile on her face, a giant armload of fragrant flowers arrayed under her nose. I knew that she was happy in her pursuit of what mattered most to her. This is what desire looks like.

DESIRE IS A VERB: DISCOVER, DECLARE, DO

The biggest challenge for women is moving desire out of their heads, letting it travel into their hearts, and then converting that heartfelt urge into meaningful, purposeful action. This can be bewildering work, because it takes awareness, tuning into where our desire lives within us, and coaxing it along toward action. Being mindful takes practice, and it takes commitment. And yet no one can be mindful all of the time. If that were possible, that person would be a robot, or a sage living on a remote mountain-top somewhere far away.

Discovering your desires requires cultivating mindfulness, a state of alert awareness. We practice this by stripping away the excesses of our lives; whether that means limiting the time we spend on the computer, eliminating processed foods from our diet, or resisting that second glass of wine, simplifying supports mindfulness.

Like my own budding meditation practice, tuning into our thoughts, noticing our self-judgments for the recordings that they are, and turning our gaze toward our desires is a lifelong project. We need to constantly clear out the clutter so we can approach reality with open eyes and an open mind. This is the only way we will break our unhelpful habits. We cannot think our way to having a better relationship with food, just as we can't conjure up a suitable partner. We have to get out there and try different things, feel our way through the experiments, and declare our discoveries. We have to be willing to do it all passionately and imperfectly.

Fulfilling our deepest desires takes some time. It's not something you can just think about; it's something you have to do.

We need to take all of this on with joy. And a sense of playfulness! For me, stepping into desire is like taking on the greatest art project of your lifetime; it's about finding out what really makes you tick and then finding the most enlivening, thrilling ways to express all that desire out in the big beautiful world, in the full light of day.

THE ULTIMATE DESIRE

Women aren't just desirable: they are desir-*ing.* When we become brave enough to shamelessly name and own our cravings, we begin to grow in gorgeously surprising ways. It's about the peeling of the feminine onion that's deep in the heart of each of us. When a woman first comes to me, her motivating desire might be to lose weight, but then, when she's on her way with that preliminary desire, she may realize that what she really wants is to be more relaxed around food, and she wants to be more relaxed around food so she feels better in her body. And she wants to feel better in her body so she's more at ease around other people. She wants to be more at ease around others because she wants closeness, connection, and intimacy. She wants a partner. A family. A community. She wants love. She wants to love and be loved so she can give the best of herself to the world around her.

Desire is the fire that lights women up. Living a life of desire means living an artful, heartfelt life. It's time for us to own this. It's time to step into our desire with our hearts on fire and our eyes wide open.

This is my invitation to you.

ACKNOWLEDGMENTS

First, I need to acknowledge the biggest inspirational rock stars for this book: my amazing clients and readers, who I counsel and coach through my website, Cravings Cleanse e-courses and mentoring programs. You are the brave ones who step into the gap between how diets have been done for too long, and what we all hope to find: a truly beautiful and healthy relationship with our bodies and food. Your vulnerability and dedication to yourselves and your desires is a gift: you call forth my inner healer, a fountain of creativity and inspiration. When I'm serving and offering you the new path to your big motivating desires, I'm alive, hopeful, and in love with the world.

To my parents, Jim and Eileen Jamieson, I adore and appreciate you beyond measure. You are my bedrock foundation. Two people could not have provided a stronger cornerstone on which to build a wildly creative, gypsylike life. Dad, you taught me that the human body and soul are capable of incredible works. Your dedication to your calling to education, guiding children to learn and grow over the years, continues to inspire me. "Thank you" seems like a paltry expression, but, from the bottom of my heart, thank you.

My siblings, cousins, aunts, uncles, and grandmothers are endless sources of playful love and inspiration. They are the smartest, most creative, caring people I know, and I love you all and can't wait to share this work with you.

Deep, loving, laughing gratitude to my friends, teachers, and inspirational guides: Brennan Wood, Jessica Ortner, Erin Stutland, Rebekah Borucki, Melissa Kathryn Farley, Ella Nemcova, Jennifer Giannettoni, Jennifer and Mike Jones, Kayce Neill, Diane Sanfilippo, and my son, Laken.

To the friends who I've masterminded with, interviewed, asked questions of, bounced ideas around with, spent endless hours strategizing and dreaming, sharing, laughing, and hoping with: Summer Bock, Terri Cole, Kavita J. Patel, Kristen Domingue, Stella Orange, Dr. Sara Gottfried, Renee Airya, Robyn Youkillis, Alison Leipzig, Heather Pierce Giannone, Danielle

Diamond, Jessica Scheer, Christina Weber, Jeannine Yoder, Rachel Tenenbaum, Michelle Goldblum, Latham Thomas, Jadah Sellner, Clay Hebert, Julia Roy, Cynthia Morris, Christina Salerno, Liz Scully, Kristoffer Carter, Karen Gordon, Maryellen Charbonneau, Stephanie Fields, Celia Slater, Heidi Nicholl, Paul Elliott, Leanne Ely, Marc David, Dr. Sara Gottfried, Robin Nielsen, Debi Silber, Cynthia Pasquella and your magical curling iron, Dr. Alan Christianson, Pedram Shojai, AJ Yager, Dr. Anna Cabeca, Mira and Dr. Jayson Calton, Pattie Ptak, Camper Bull, Dr. Tom O'Bryan, Cora Poage, Lindsay Wilson, Sirena Bernal, Jennifer Blackstock, Cassie Price, Sara Davidson, Kristen Bates, Carolyn Messere, Kristina Shands, Lois Wong, Allison Rutberg, Laura Dinstell, Ginny Johnson, Sara Mazenko, Sora No, Jeannine Yoder, Emily Rosen, Danielle LaPorte, Kris Carr, Kate Northrup, Christina Rasmussen, and Michael Parrish Dudell.

My inspirational coaches, JJ Virgin, Jonathan Fields, Monica Shah, Ariel and Shya Kane, and Nisha Moodley. Thank you for seeing and holding a bigger vision for this book and me as we morphed and grew, and became this force of nature.

To my awesome support team: so much

love and gratitude. Thanks to Luska Joseph for picking my son up from school, and my amazing assistants, Jan Udlock and Janice Formichella.

This book would not be possible without the sweet support of my agent, Wendy Sherman. From our first phone call after you saw my interview with Jonathan Fields, through our happy dance in the elevator down from our meeting at Simon & Schuster, it has been a fun pleasure. Thanks also to Tricia Boczkowski, my brilliant, adorable editor at Gallery Books. Every meeting is filled with smiles and I love that this book came to you.

A heartfelt thanks to my editor and co-writer, Emily Heckman. Our walks up the Malibu canyons were an inspiration. This book blossomed as a collaboration and it wouldn't be what it is without you.

Finally, to my partner in life, Bob: without you, I never would have had the courage to "come out of the vegan closet," nor would I have weathered the storm that followed. Your love and dedication, care and brilliant mind are huge sources of comfort and inspiration. I love you, and how you constantly hold the space for me to discover and follow my desires.